T0294620

Museum Gallery Activities

American Alliance of Museums

The American Alliance of Museums (AAM) has been bringing museums together since 1906, helping to develop standards and best practices, gathering and sharing knowledge, and providing advocacy on issues of concern to the entire museum community. Representing more than 35,000 individual museum professionals and volunteers, institutions, and corporate partners serving the museum field, the Alliance stands for the broad scope of the museum community.

The American Alliance of Museums' mission is to champion museums and nurture excellence in partnership with its members and allies.

Books published by AAM further the Alliance's mission to make standards and best practices for the broad museum community widely available.

Museum Gallery Activities

A Handbook

Sharon Vatsky

ROWMAN & LITTLEFIELD
Lanham • Boulder • New York • London

Published by Rowman & Littlefield
An imprint of The Rowman & Littlefield Publishing Group, Inc.
4501 Forbes Boulevard, Suite 200, Lanham, Maryland 20706
www.rowman.com

Unit A, Whitacre Mews, 26-34 Stannary Street, London SE11 4AB, United Kingdom

British Library Cataloguing in Publication Information Available

Library of Congress Cataloging-in-Publication Data

Names: Vatsky, Sharon, author. | American Alliance of Museums, issuing body.
Title: Museum gallery activities : a handbook / Sharon Vatsky.
Description: Lanham : Rowman & Littlefield, [2018] | "American Alliance of Museums." | Includes bibliographical references.
Identifiers: LCCN 2018007118 (print) | LCCN 2018025372 (ebook) | ISBN 9781538108659 (Electronic) | ISBN 9781538108635 | ISBN 9781538108635 (cloth : alk. paper) | ISBN 9781538108642 (paperback : alk. paper)
Subjects: LCSH: Art museum visitors—Services for. | Art--Study and teaching—Activity programs.
Classification: LCC N435 (ebook) | LCC N435 .V38 2018 (print) | DDC 069/.1—dc23
LC record available at https://lccn.loc.gov/2018007118

♾™ The paper used in this publication meets the minimum requirements of American National Standard for Information Sciences—Permanence of Paper for Printed Library Materials, ANSI/NISO Z39.48-1992.

Printed in the United States of America

For my family family, and my museum family

Contents

List of Illustrations

List of Illustrations

*Denotes that more information and a color image of this work of art can be found at the Collection Online https://www.guggenheim .org/collection-online

Preface

For those of you who come to this book as art museum educators, you are probably already familiar with the term "gallery activity."[1] At the Solomon R. Guggenheim Museum where I have worked since 2000, I am part of a teaching community that specializes in creating and facilitating gallery experiences for students, families, teachers, youth, and adults. Over the years we have developed a planning framework for building these experiences (also known as tours) that includes choosing a tour theme, carefully selecting and sequencing artworks, and using inquiry-based questions to prompt discussions. However, when a new exhibition opens at the museum, we are invariably most excited about developing and sharing new gallery activities.

For the uninitiated, the term *gallery activity* is used to denote the segments of a guided museum tour where participants *do* something. Tour participants may be asked to debate a point, take a pose, respond to music, author a poem, or create a collage with the intent of gaining deeper insights and personal connections to a work of art. The gallery activity may be structured so that you work on your own or collaboratively with other members of the group. What joins all of these activities together is the opportunity to respond to a work of art through modalities other than discussion with the aim of prompting new perspectives and insights.

In my experience, museum visitors welcome this participatory opportunity. Yes, they want to look together and talk about the works of art they ponder, but as most museum educators have discovered for themselves, within most groups you will have some who are eager to talk and share their insights, but there are others who prefer to hang back, reluctant to contribute to the conversation. Not every visitor has the confidence to voice their opinion.

People learn in different ways—some love to talk, others are mortified by the idea of speaking up. Some are confident in drawing; others will feel uneasy when asked to sketch. Some are "naturals" when it comes to recreating the pose of a figure in a portrait painting, while others will be self-conscious. We all have comfort and discomfort areas and individual learning styles, but the addition of gallery activities can provide multiple ways to get everyone to participate in the process of connecting deeply with works of art.

This is perhaps too obvious to dwell on, but the term *gallery* means that the activity happens within the physical confines of the exhibitions on view. The work of art is in close proximity and beckoning us to make further connections. Having said that "gallery activities" happen in galleries, I will quickly add that they are also extremely useful in a classroom setting. I am aware that this sounds like a contradiction. Whenever you are looking at a work of art, whether in original form in a museum or a projected reproduction in a classroom, gallery activities have the potential to connect viewers with the art they are looking at more deeply. Everyone on you tour (or in your classroom) is invited to participate at the same time. This simultaneous participation means that everyone is engaged in the activity. The goal is not to be "the best," but rather to respond in your own unique and valid way, and contribute to the cumulative process of meaning-making.

Gallery activities encourage us to flex aspects of our responsive abilities that are less utilized. Western thought has tended to value verbal and written communication over other ways of perceiving. According to Olga Hubard, associate professor of art education, Teachers College, Columbia University, "Discursive language in both its written and spoken forms, has been the dominant mode in formal education for centuries. In fact, some people have become accustomed to thinking of words as the sole carriers of 'true' knowledge. Perhaps for this reason, non-discursive modes of mediation are not always given the seriousness they deserve."[2]

Although gallery activities are commonly used with younger audiences, one of the major premises of this book is that thoughtfully designed gallery activities can and should be incorporated into learning experiences for audiences of all ages and abilities. At the Guggenheim, activities are woven into every tour from stroller tours for babies and their caregivers to tours for adult visitors. Of course, this doesn't mean that toddlers and seniors participate in the same gallery activities, but rather that developmentally appropriate gallery activities are incorporated into museum experiences across all of our audiences. This unified approach recognizes that active learning is a valid and productive strategy for supporting deeper and more memorable connections to works of art for visitors of all ages.

At the Guggenheim, we have many programs where participants explore the exhibitions and then head to the art studios in another part of the museum to create their own work. Inspired by the art they have seen, they may create a work that uses a similar theme, process, or art material, but once they are outside the exhibition, participants are creating their own work—moving away from the work of art by a well-known artist, toward considering their own ideas and how to express them. Gallery activities can provide a perfect "bridge" between carefully considering works in an exhibition and turning one's attention to creating one's own art in a studio setting, but they are not the same. Gallery activities are usually characterized by their relatively short duration, limited materials, spontaneity, and impromptu approach. The emphasis is on the experience rather than the product. In the hands of a skilled educator, the gallery activity and the art project can provide complementary opportunities for exploration and discovery.

Gallery activities are not a new phenomenon. In researching this book, I found articles dating back to the early 1970s that advocate for active learning and participation. Yes, the research of the time focuses almost exclusively on involving younger students, but the descriptions of some of the activities are nearly identical to ones that you will find on the pages of this book.[3] In 1972, Susan Sollins wrote, "Through the use of games, children in a museum can be encouraged to look carefully at things around them, to use their eyes. Without discussion, it can become clear to each child that his reactions are important and valid."[4]

And yet there is a new urgency calling for museums to revamp the experiences they offer to visitors. As I write this book, I see almost daily news about museums devoting substantial resources toward making their museums more interactive. A recent headline from the *Boston Globe* heralds, "Peabody Essex Museum Hires Neuroscientist to Enhance Visitor Experience." The article goes on to state, "What we want to create is a sense of exploration and discovery. It's to get people out of the mode of interacting with art on an unconscious level and beginning to think about what's going on in the paintings."[5] In an effort to keep audiences returning in a world that offers evermore options for leisure time pursuits, museums are focusing on creating interactive learning opportunities.

With all the current focus on interactivity it is surprising that this book has not already been written. Each time I conduct a workshop, those participating request printed handouts of the gallery activities that were part of the museum tour. Over the years I have accumulated multiple handouts, not only from the tours, workshops, and courses that I have conducted, but also those from programs that my colleagues have presented at conferences across the country. It seemed to me it was time to gather up all of these ideas and organize them into a form that can be both a compendium, and hopefully, a motivation for developing new activities.

Most of the activities that are included in this book have been selected because they have the potential to be used in conjunction with many different works of art. Although you will find examples of artworks from the Guggenheim's collection, this book is written with the intention that these ideas will be freely adapted for your personal teaching style, and to support the works in your exhibitions and collections.

Figure Preface.1. Museum educator Megan Lucas facilitates a gallery conversation.

I have been fortunate to have the opportunity to work with museum educators, docents, and teachers both domestically and internationally. Time and again I have been told that they are being asked by their supervisors to be more interactive and inquiry-based in their teaching, but many are not receiving concrete professional development programs to implement these goals. And so, this handbook is written as a practical guide that focuses on a particular aspect of tour planning and facilitation.

This book is written for the practitioner and emphasizes the "what" and "how" over the "why." If you are a seasoned educator, I expect that you will skip directly to the second part of this volume to look for new activities to try out. I am not offended. It is exactly the way I would delve into this book. You have already learned that gallery activities can add a powerful and positive ingredient to your tours. For those newer to incorporating gallery activities into your teaching, part I of this book will provide a foundation, rationale, and guidelines for constructing activities.

When I begin workshops about gallery teaching, I frequently use this photograph (figure Preface.1) as my first slide. It shows a fairly typical weekday morning at the Guggenheim Museum with students looking at and discussing a work of art with a skilled gallery educator (in this case Megan Lucas) facilitating a conversation. The thing that strikes me about this photo is not the engagement of the young people—that is fairly standard, but rather the look on the face of the young man in the CAL POLY t-shirt. If I could put a "thought bubble" over his head, I imagine it might read, "What are these kids seeing that I'm missing?" The influential social psychologist Mihalyi Csikszentmihalyi seems to agree:

> Total immersion in the work of art is the magic experts and laypersons alike hope for when they visit a museum, but rarely attain . . . Yet most potential museum visitors just do not know what they are supposed to do in front of a work of art. [They] are very aware that they sorely lack the background for getting the full benefit of what they are exposed to.[6]

This book is about offering visitors some possible pathways to connecting to works of art through their senses. Participation in gallery activities encourages visitors to spend more time with works of art, consider them more closely, and bring their knowledge and experiences to the task of creating personal meaning. By sitting together in front of works of art, talking about them, and exploring them with all our senses, I sincerely believe that gallery activities can offer a path toward "total immersion" and allow for deeper and more authentic connections with works of art.

Acknowledgments

I have had this book in my head for a long time. The more I observed, participated in, and developed gallery activities, the more I thought these ideas should be documented and made available in a single useable handbook that could serve as a handy reference. Although it has been my task to pull these disparate ideas together into a single volume, the content has come from many sources, and I am indebted to those who have contributed and supported this project.

Over my long tenure as a museum educator, I have been privileged to work with many extraordinary museum educators. This is a generous profession that values collaboration and sharing. It would be nearly impossible to mention all the dedicated and creative museum educators I have worked with during my nearly thirty years in the field. When I remember where and how a particular activity came into my awareness, I have noted and acknowledged the source. In many cases however, I cannot recall exactly when I added each activity to the collective "toolbox." I have acquired many of these activities seemingly by osmosis. Some activities are adapted from my years as an art teacher in public schools and as an instructor teaching drawing and design at the college level. Others are inspired directly by the artists, materials, processes, and curatorial premises in exhibitions on view in our galleries. I have tried to compile a list of names, but every time I do, I am worried about leaving someone important out. So if you are reading this and thinking, "I wonder if Sharon included me in the acknowledgments?" Yes, I did! Thank you!

Since 2001, I have worked with Kim Kanatani, deputy director, and Gail Engelberg director of education at the Guggenheim. Kanatani's leadership has laid the ground work for creating a consistent methodology across the education department that encourages the inclusion of visitor voices and participatory museum experiences. She has also provided me with the flexibility to write this book. My colleagues in the education department, Alyson Luck and Greer Kudon, have offered consistent encouragement and support. No museum educator is an expert in every modality, and so when it came to writing the chapter on digital media activities, I contacted Rebecca Mir, my former colleague at the Guggenheim, who eagerly reviewed and contributed to the chapter. I could not have asked for a more perfect collaborator.

I am grateful to Kim Bush, director of licensing and traveling exhibitions at the Guggenheim who facilitated permissions for the works of art from the museum's collection to be reproduced on the pages of this book.

Thank you to the American Alliance of Museums publications division who recognized that a book on gallery activities could be of interest to their members, and to Charles Harmon, executive editor; Katie O'Brien, associate editor; Michael Tan, editorial assistant; and Chris Fischer, associate editor, production at Rowman & Littlefield for their guidance in moving this book toward publication.

Over the years I have had the opportunity to work with many promising students and talented colleagues and in the spirit of the wonderful and generous museum educators who have shared their ideas with me, I encourage you to use and adapt the activities in this book and especially invite you to create new ones.

Part I

Chapter 1

Who This Book Was Written For

"Our job is to connect the familiar to the unfamiliar, and in doing so, ignite a passion for how diverse, exciting, and essential art [or history, or science] can be." —Nina Simon,[1] executive director of the Santa Cruz Museum of Art & History and author of *The Participatory Museum* and *The Art of Relevance*

Having spent a good part of my career working in museum education departments, I know that museum educators who facilitate participatory gallery experiences for visitors are, of course, a primary target audience for this book. However, I truly believe that the addition of gallery activities to one's repertoire of teaching strategies is something that can benefit a much broader swath of educators. I am using the term "gallery activities" because it is the most common terminology, but it is truly a misnomer. The activities described in this book are equally useful and applicable to learning environments outside of museums. I have written this book with many potential "users" in mind.

K–12 Art Museum Gallery Educators

For those intrepid, creative souls who spend their days shepherding school groups through art museums, my hope is that some of the gallery activities in this book will already be in your toolbox, but that you will also find variations that you will want to try and be inspired to create new ones. As in any lesson plan or teaching suggestion, the approach should be adjusted to your particular teaching style, audience, and goals.

Art Museum Educators Who Work with Families

Gallery activities are a mainstay of family programs. Getting adults and kids to collaborate and participate in response to encounters with works of art are central programmatic goals for family audiences. At the Guggenheim, gallery activities are a major part of how family members connect to the art they view and to each other.

Art Museum Educators Who Work with Youth with Disabilities

Gallery activities are at the core of the experiences you create. Instead of focusing the museum experience exclusively through words, adaptive gallery activities provide alternative strategies for making connections with works of art.

Gallery activities allow participants to respond at their own level—not a single, one-size-fits-all solution but flexible approaches that have the elasticity to accommodate individual aptitudes.[2] From prekindergarten to graduate school, classrooms include students with diverse physical, sensory, and learning abilities. Gallery activities meet the needs of diverse learners by providing varied ways to respond to works of art. They do this by providing options for the following:

- Presenting information and content in different ways

- Differentiating the ways that young people can express what they know

- Stimulating interest and motivation for learning

Art Museum Educators Who Work with Adults with Disabilities

Multimodal gallery activities enable adults with disabilities to participate fully in museum experiences. Educators will be able to maximize capabilities and minimize disability in planning tours. At the Guggenheim, our program, *Mind's Eye,* serves adults with low vision and blindness. Verbal descriptions, touch objects, tactile materials, props, and art making can work toward compensating for visual acuity and provide alternative ways to perceive and engage with works of art.

Art Museum Educators Who Work with School-Based Teachers

This is my primary audience. Educators come to the museum's exhibitions and learn strategies that they can take back to the classroom. In my experience they are eager to participate and game for anything! They are brave and look to you to provide ways of connecting with art and the curriculum that will resonate with their students. You will also learn from their experience and insights.

Art Museum Educators Who Work with Adult Audiences

Although it is common for gallery activities to be incorporated into museum experiences for younger audiences, I emphatically urge you to incorporate them into your adult tours as well. At the Guggenheim, adult tours are usually peppered with opportunities for inquiry-based discussions and drawing and/or writing activities. Because some of our educators work with both younger and adult visitors, K–12 strategies have percolated up to adult programming and proved exceedingly successful. We now have an integrated teaching philosophy that is consistent from our stroller tours for babies and their caregivers through adult touring experiences.

This doesn't mean that we use the same activities for adults that we do for younger visitors. What it does mean is that we have realized that active learning is a sound strategy for all ages.

Museum Educators in History and Science Museums

The commonality between all museums and museum educators is belief in the power of teaching with objects—whether the "object" is a painting, a dinosaur skeleton, or an historical document.

Many of the activities outlined here can be adapted to serve teaching goals in history and science museums.

K–12 Art Teachers

Until I began working in art museums, I had never heard of or thought about gallery activities. In studio art classes (where I worked for many years), the art teacher introduced a medium, theme, or concept and then invited students to create their own work. In my days as a K–8 art teacher, there was less emphasis on introducing works by well-known artists, and art history was thought to be inappropriate for students younger than high school level.

Times have changed. Well-known artists are routinely introduced to students at a very early age, and gallery activities can be a useful and creative "bridge" between an in-depth consideration of a work of art and individual student expression.

Despite the misnomer, gallery activities can and should be an important addition to the classroom art curriculum. Art teachers are now required to not only motivate students to create their own art, but also to become knowledgeable in art history and develop both oral and written literacy skills. Many of the gallery activities described in this book will be equally valuable and applicable in the classroom. A few of them actually work better in the classroom than in the galleries.

Teachers of Art History and Art Appreciation

For several years, before my museum education career began, I taught art history and art appreciation at the college level. How I wish I had known about these techniques then! At that time, I still followed the basic lecturing model: show a slide, read the object label, provide a bit of commentary, then on to the next slide.

From my informal surveys of current college-level students, most college art history classes are still taught this way. The job of the student is to take notes; memorize artist's names, titles of works, and dates; and recount these facts on tests. I want to go back and teach those classes with the addition of inquiry-based discussions and gallery activities. It would be a whole new experience for me and the students.

The addition of multimodal activities to art history classes and art appreciation classes will deepen students' personal connections to works of art, make them more memorable, and make classes more varied and engaging.

Teachers of Subject Areas Other Than Visual Arts

If you teach language arts or social studies, these activities will resonate with your curriculum. Although this is not a book about using works of art to improve literacy skills, regularly talking and writing about works of art has been demonstrated to support these competencies.[3] Teachers of history and social studies can think about works of art as primary documents that show us the concerns, aspirations, and everyday moments of past and current generations.

Although it is somewhat more difficult to create authentic correlations with science and mathematics curricula, these suggestions are relevant but may require a bit of tweaking. Many museums have created website interfaces that allow teachers to search the museum's collection and locate works that will relate to their subject area.

Teachers of Adult English Language Learners

Using visual art is the perfect prompt to get adults talking, writing, and developing language skills. I am frequently gratified when a member of an adult English language learner (ELL) class starts their contribution to the activity by saying, "I said to myself that I wasn't going to talk because my English isn't good, but I have to say . . . " Gallery activities can be used to get students active in their acquisition of and confidence in using language. They also encourage ELLs to fully participate by using modalities other than talking and writing.

Museum Education Students

For more than a decade, I taught a graduate course in museum education. The course took place at the Guggenheim Museum, and the "final" was to present an interactive, thematic tour—including gallery activities. Some of the gallery activities included in this book were devised by my former students. If your chosen field is museum education, getting comfortable with gallery teaching and multimodal approaches to interpretation will prove vital and rewarding as you continue along your professional path.

Chapter 2

Where Gallery Activities Fit in Planning a Tour

"I thought this program would be about teaching art, instead it has turned out to be about the art of teaching."[1]

In 2005, the Guggenheim Museum began a collaboration with the Metropolitan Museum of Art, Museum of Modern Art, and Whitney Museum of American Art to develop an annual summer teacher institute called Connecting Collections: Integrating Modern and Contemporary Art into the Classroom.[2] Each July, this weeklong professional development program brings together forty educators from all subject areas who teach grades 3–12. Although many of the teachers are from the New York metropolitan area, the program also attracts teachers from across the United States and abroad.

This work with our partner institutions has yielded an intensive program focused on sharing gallery teaching practices. Planning the program together has necessitated that we fully discuss the teaching methodology at each museum and come to an agreement about best practices and the teaching model we will share with program participants.[3]

Although the four museums are sometimes perceived as having different teaching philosophies, as staff members from the education departments came together and began to discuss our teaching methods and philosophy, we discovered that we were essentially on the same page and in basic agreement about the methods and structure that yield effective gallery teaching. We all agreed that it was useful to organize gallery tours thematically, facilitate inquiry-based discussions, add relevant contextual information, and include multimodal activities—or gallery activities—to provide further learning opportunities. We realized that what might be construed as separate methodologies are more manifestations of personal style. After many long discussions we agreed on a lesson plan structure that would be flexible enough to allow for different teaching styles, interests, and content and still produce compelling, participatory tours. The structure we agreed on includes four steps to creating a gallery experience. It can be stretched and molded and still retains its ability to provide a clear structure around which an engaging tour can be fashioned.

Tours Are Thematic

One of the main areas of agreement is that *thematic* tours allow the museum educator to "curate" the gallery experience and tailor it to the interests and developmental level of the group they will be working with. A thematic structure allows the educator to select works that are appropriate for their group and support their teaching goals. Despite the richness and depth of the exhibitions at our institutions, we do not focus on touring any single exhibition; rather, we select a theme and three to five works of art that fall under a thematic umbrella.

Some examples of tried and true themes include identity: society and politics; spaces and places; nature; narrative; everyday objects; transformation; conflict; and artist choices. We look for broad, jargon-free themes. The individual works of art selected for the tour may be very different from one another but share a common thematic thread. In order to make the theme as generally accessible as possible we avoid "art terms"; for instance, selecting the theme of *people*, rather than *portraits*; *places* rather than *landscapes*.

To further clarify what we mean by *theme,* we have elaborated a set of criteria. A teaching theme is

- A universal lens that is relevant to students' lives and classroom content

- Either immediately, or through exploration, visually evident in the work of art

- A concept that can be explored in depth and on many levels

- A common point of connection through which to frame the objects

We also consider *object selection* and *sequencing*. What are the best works to choose to support your theme, and what is the best order in which to present them? Although not a hard-and-fast rule, we have found that beginning with a more concrete, figurative, or narrative work, and saving the most abstract, conceptual, or challenging work for last, is frequently a good strategy. This approach allows those on your tour to begin with ideas and images that are more familiar and concrete. Having participated in lively discussions and built confidence at the beginning of the tour, participants become more willing to tackle works with increasing ambiguity.

Below is a set of criteria to further clarify this approach to object (artwork) selection and se-quencing. Objects

- Relate clearly to the theme

- Are sequenced to allow for a greater understanding of the theme throughout the lesson

- Address the theme in a variety of ways

- Are developmentally appropriate

A good way to begin planning a new tour is by spending extended time in your galleries. Look for connections between works that are on view, but also for unexpected ways that a work of art can relate to the theme. Choosing a clear, simple theme and communicating it to the group you are working with helps to orient the group and focus your conversations.

Creating thematic tours provides an added degree of transparency. Participants on the tour understand why you may be stopping at one work rather than another and can access their own experiences and expertise within the chosen theme.

Themes, however, should not be rigidly enforced. At times the conversations in front of artworks may meander away from the theme, but if the conversation strays too far afield, having a theme allows the educator to regroup and refocus.

Tours Use Effective Questions to Elicit Responses

The use of carefully constructed, open-ended questions is a cornerstone of gallery teaching. If a question is truly inquiry-based and open-ended, there will be many possible interesting and compelling responses. Developing thought-provoking questions is not as easy as it might seem. Questions include those that require observation: "What do you notice?"; those that activate prior knowledge such as, "What does this remind you of?"; as well as those that encourage interpretation: "How is this similar or different from the previous work that we saw?"

As we focus on works in the galleries, dialogue is encouraged through the strategic use of open-ended questions. Participants notice details, propose examples, look for evidence, and consider ideas, theories, and speculations in response to open-ended questions.

We use this checklist to help assess whether questions are open-ended:

- Questions invite multiple responses

- Encourage close looking and critical thinking

- Support the theme and lesson goals

- Are sequenced from observation to interpretation

Information Is Inserted into the Discussion in Response to Observations and Comments from Participants

How do you ensure that participants are also provided with important information about the works of art on which they are focusing? As museum professionals and museum-goers, we have experienced tours that run the gamut of approaches. On one end, there is a method that depends solely on the delivery of information from the "expert" tour guide. This traditional method is still used in many museums and supposes learning can be transmitted by simply recounting what you know to a captive audience. On the other end of the spectrum is the belief that information about a work of art gets in the way of close looking.

We believe that viewers want to look closely and make their own discoveries, but they also have the expectation that they will learn something new and come away with a greater understanding of the works of art on which they are focusing.

Contextual information can be layered into art-focused discussions. Information is inserted in response to participant observations or questions with the goal of moving the discussion to a deeper level. *Not all information is equal.* On one hand, some information, for instance, such as where the artist studied or a list of her or his exhibitions, will most likely not be retained because it is extrinsic to the artwork, the theme, and the conversation. On the other hand, information inserted in response to an observation or question that a participant contributes can support greater understanding and learning. This means that the educator should have a thorough knowledge of all the works they are exploring, because at any moment an observation, question, or comment may be posited that will provide an "opening" for a piece of information to be inserted. This situation has been dubbed a "teachable moment" where the participant's curiosity creates an opportunity to insert relevant information that may provide new insights and move the conversation to a deeper level. Contextual information is most effective when it is integrated into the discussion, is relevant to the conversation, and

- Supports exploration of the theme

- Aligns with the lesson goals

- May take various forms including artist quotes, photographs, primary documents or video clips

Tours Include Gallery Activities/Multimodal Activities

So where do gallery activities fit in this structure?

Here we consider approaches beyond dialogue that can support learning. Participants experience ways to respond to works of art through activities such as drawing, movement, sound, and writing. The rest of this book is devoted to developing this aspect of a gallery experience.

In general, a gallery activity is planned for each stop on the tour. Activities can be short—writing down a single word, passing around a touch object, or taking a pose, but at other tour stops the educator might dedicate significant time to the multimodal activity such as doing a longer drawing or writing activity. The length of your tour and attention span of your group will dictate how long you will stop at each work and devote to each activity.

Although most museum educators will initiate a tour stop with an open-ended conversation before introducing a multimodal activity, an activity can be inserted at any point in a tour stop as long as there is a rationale for why this is the best moment to introduce this activity.

Putting Activities at the Beginning

Here are some activities that might lead off a tour stop.

- Write down a single word that comes to mind when you look at this work.

- Write down the title you would give to this work.

- Take a moment to sketch a detail from this work that interests you.

These prompts can be conversation starters and provide a moment at the beginning of the tour stop to collect one's thoughts.

In the Middle of a Tour Stop

These are activities that might be inserted in the middle of a tour stop.

- Take the pose of the person in the painting/sculpture

- Choose a brush and create a brush stroke (in the air) that you see in the painting

- Pass around a touch object that relates to the work

Inserting an activity in the middle of a tour stop can prompt additional insights and discussions.

Activities and the End of a Tour Stop

These are activities that might done at the end of a tour stop.

- A collaborative poem

- An annotated drawing

- A written postcard to a friend or relative that shares your experience of this work

- An opportunity to reflect on what has been seen and learned

During the course of the weeklong program, participating educators have the opportunity to select and sequence works of art, formulate open-ended questions, research relevant information, and create gallery activities. By the conclusion of the program, each educator has created a lesson plan that will become part of their curriculum when they return to school. With a few adjustments, this lesson plan template can be used to create gallery tours or lessons taught in the classroom.[4]

Combining these tour-building elements enables the educator to create an experience that is unique, flexible, and yet grounded in an underlying structure that can be applied to constructing vastly different lessons and gallery experiences.

Chapter 3

How Gallery Activities Support Learning and Connections with Works of Art

"One must learn by doing the thing, for though you think you know it—you have no certainty until you try." —Sophocles, fifth century BC

For more than a decade, I taught a graduate course in museum education at the City University of New York. On the first day of class, I would ask students to recall their best educational experience, share it with the group, and identify what characteristics made this such a positive learning experience.

Invariably, students would recall travel trips abroad, wilderness programs, learning a new skill, or a special teacher who knew how to make learning exciting. Students used words like *challenging, collaborative, supportive, experimental, exploratory, unique,* and *engaging* to recall these special learning environments. Try it for yourself and see what comes to mind and the qualities associated with that special learning experience.

Across the field of education, it is now generally accepted that students retain more knowledge when they are actively engaged in the process of learning. Both educational theory and research support what many of us have noticed in our own educational process—that active involvement in learning is more durable, enjoyable, and memorable than passive listening. Below are some current educational theories that strongly support the idea that being an effective museum educator requires that you commit to incorporating multimodal gallery activities into your teaching.

Active Learning

Active learning is anything that involves visitors in doing things and thinking about the things they are doing.[1] The core elements of active learning are participant activity and engagement in the learning process. Active learning is often contrasted with the traditional lecture format where information is passively received from the instructor. Since research suggests that audience attention begins to wane every ten to twenty minutes, incorporating active learning techniques into your teaching encourages prolonged engagement. The learning needs of the participants are at the center of active learning. The benefits of using activities include improved critical thinking skills, increased retention and transfer of new information, increased motivation, and improved interpersonal skills.[2]

"Bear in mind that the most compelling learning experiences are all-encompassing. All of an individual's sensory channels become engaged in the experience, reducing competing information without reducing complexity. Such all-encompassing experiences provide a sharper focus and a more memorable experience. This is why multi-channel/multimodal learning works; it is learning through all the senses."[3]

Multiple Intelligences

Dr. Howard Gardner, a psychologist and professor of neuroscience at Harvard University, developed the theory of multiple intelligences (MI) in 1983. The theory challenged traditional beliefs in the fields of education and cognitive science.[4]

According to Gardner, human beings have at least eight different kinds of intelligence that reflect different ways of interacting with the world. Each person has a unique combination or profile. Although we each have all eight intelligences, no two individuals have them in the same exact configuration.

Gardner proposed that human beings have evolved to be able to carry out at least eight separate forms of analysis:

1. Linguistic intelligence ("word smart")

2. Logical-mathematical intelligence ("number/reasoning smart")

3. Spatial intelligence ("picture smart")

4. Bodily-kinesthetic intelligence ("body smart")

5. Musical intelligence ("music smart")

6. Interpersonal intelligence ("people smart")

7. Intrapersonal intelligence ("self smart")

8. Naturalist intelligence ("nature smart")

One of the most remarkable features of this theory of multiple intelligences is that it provides multiple pathways to learning, and not only suggests but demands that we vary our teaching modalities and expand our horizon of available teaching/learning tools beyond the conventional linguistic approaches.

Constructivism

Constructivism is a theory based on observation and scientific study that states that people construct their own understanding and knowledge of the world through experiencing things and reflecting on those experiences. Instead of being passive recipients of information, we are active creators of our own knowledge. Writers and researchers in many areas of education draw upon the work of such educational psychologists as John Dewey, Jean Piaget, and Lev Vigotsky in formulating Constructivism.

In his book *Learning in the Museum* (1998), George Hein writes that visitors construct knowledge by making connections between their lives and the objects they encounter in the museum.[5] The curatorial goals of an exhibition may be very different from the meanings that individual visitors come away with.

Constructivist theory asserts that prior knowledge is of primary importance. Rather than learners being empty vessels into which information can be poured, they come to museums with a wealth of knowledge and experiences. It is upon this existing knowledge that new meaning is constructed.

Constructivist educational theory puts forth that in any discussion of teaching and learning the focus needs to be on the learner, not on the subject to be learned. For museums, this suggests that our primary focus should be on the visitor, not the exhibition content. By understanding the Constructivist theory of learning, we can develop museum experiences that respond to the uniqueness of our visitors and maximize the potential for learning. The Constructivist museum recognizes that knowledge is created in the mind of the learner using personal learning methods. It encourages us to acknowledge and accommodate the diversity of our visitors.[6]

Brain Research

Our brains are designed to be attracted to novelty. Anything that is new, different, or unusual will arouse interest, and astute educators can use this innate attraction to novelty to provoke and deepen learning.

Psychologists have long known that when we experience a novel situation within a familiar context, we are more likely to remember that event. Recent studies of the brain have begun to explain how this process happens and to suggest new ways of teaching that could improve learning and memory.

There is a region in our brain that responds to novel stimuli. One of the most important brain regions involved in discovering, processing, and storing new sensory impressions is the hippocampus, located in the temporal lobe of the cerebral cortex. Novel stimuli tend to activate the hippocampus more than familiar stimuli do, which is why the hippocampus serves as the brain's "novelty detector."[7]

Contrast something you do daily, like a commute to work, with traveling to a location you have never visited before. To reach the new location, your brain needs to work much harder. It requires paying greater attention to directions and a degree of uncertainty. During this process, the brain actually forms new connections. This is why one definition of learning can be just doing something you have never done before.

This attraction to the new or novel probably evolved from early humans who needed to be aware of any changes in their environment to protect themselves from danger. As educators, this research suggests that whatever novel, unique, surprising strategies we can incorporate into our teaching are the most likely to be retained.

In addition, researchers have shown that experiences that are infused with emotional content are more memorable. Although we are accustomed to focusing on the cognitive factors involved in learning, social, emotional, and physical factors are also important. Social interactions including discussions, debates, collaborations, storytelling, group activities, and games help us process information and give it meaning. By utilizing these methods, we can ensure that learning engages all the senses and taps the emotional side of the brain.[8]

Conclusion

This is not a book about brain research or educational theory, yet current research implores us to broaden the methods we use in our teaching to include multimodal gallery activities. Research and education theory suggest that multimodal teaching should be integral to all teaching—not just as an add-on or an embellishment, but that it be at the very core of facilitating memorable museum experiences for all of our visitors.

Chapter 4

Guidelines for Creating Successful Gallery Activities

"Learning is experience. Everything else is just information." —Albert Einstein[1]

"I cannot teach anybody anything. I can only make them think." —Socrates[2]

A well-planned and facilitated gallery activity can help to make new and indelible connections between the viewer and a work of art, but I have also seen well-intended gallery activities go terribly wrong due to myriad problems. It is therefore important not only to provide a compendium of "tried and true" activities that you will find in part II of this book, but also suggest guidelines and planning procedures to ensure that newly created activities will be successful. The following checklist helps me to envision whether a new idea for a gallery activity will engage visitors or fall flat. These guidelines can be used to gauge the potential for success of a new activity before trying it out on real-live museum visitors.

Successful Gallery Activities

Put Visitors at Ease

If you work in a museum, it is easy to forget that they can be formidable and intimidating places for first-time visitors. Because the surroundings have become familiar to us, it may be hard to put ourselves in the role of that visitor being confronted with lots of information and sensory input. Everything is new and can be disorienting. Think of your own emotional state when you are visiting a place you have never been to or embarking on a task you have never tried. Think about what you would need to get oriented, comfortable, and ready to learn. The more your needs are met and your questions answered, the less anxiety you feel, and the more you will be able to concentrate on the content of the tour.

In her 2001 article, longtime museum professional Judy Rand reflects on a rafting trip through the Grand Canyon, which helped her see the needs of the visitor in a new light. She recounts her feelings of frustration and confusion as she engages in a new experience and has distilled her realizations into a set of guidelines.

I suggest that every museum educator not only read the article but also reflect on the times you felt overwhelmed or confused in a new situation. Rand presents a "Visitors' Bill of Rights," that reminds museums, exhibit planners, designers, directors, architects, and evaluators (and I will add educators), to put visitors first.[3]

1. Comfort: "Meet my basic needs."

2. Orientation: "Make it easy for me to find my way around."

3. Welcome/belonging: "Make me feel welcome."

4. Enjoyment: "I want to have fun."

5. Socializing: "I came to spend time with family and friends."

6. Respect: "Accept me for who I am and what I know."

7. Communication: "Help me understand, and let me talk, too."

8. Learning: "I want to learn something new."

9. Choice and control: "Let me choose; give me some control."

10. Challenge and confidence: "Give me a challenge I know I can handle."

11. Revitalization: "Help me leave refreshed and restored."

Interactive tours that combine conversation with activities have the potential to meet every one of these requirements. The visitors that opt in for guided gallery experiences are already seeking out a level of engagement that exceeds the typical visitor. They are committing sixty to ninety minutes of their time and trusting you to deliver a worthwhile experience. They could have chosen the "free-range" version of a visit, but instead they have chosen to spend their time with a museum educator. So you not only have a participant who has made the choice to spend their valuable free time at your institution, perhaps paying a fee to get in the door, but also one who is also willing to commit time to a guided learning experience. You are one lucky educator, but you are also tasked with a major responsibility! Having made the decision to join your tour, what are they hoping for and how can you ensure that it is provided?

In 1943, the psychologist Abraham Maslow (1908–1970) laid out a hierarchy of human behavioral needs and motivations, starting with the most basic of physical needs—shelter, food, water, safety—before advancing to higher-order needs like relationships, curiosity, and self-actualization.[4] In Maslow's hierarchy, the needs on the lower levels must be met before it is possible to fulfill higher-level needs. If the individuals with whom you are working are physically uncomfortable or emotionally uneasy, it will be difficult for them to focus on any endeavor. People don't stop having physical needs just because you have created a cool gallery activity.

A major factor in determining whether or not a participatory tour will be successful or not is the educator's ability to create a welcoming, inclusive, and respectful environment where participants genuinely feel that their ideas—even or especially those who are not regular museum goers—are welcomed into the learning space.

The museum educator has a giant task here. You are frequently working with people you are meeting for the first time. They may not have extensive knowledge of visual art or art history and may not necessarily be fluent English speakers. Some may have physical impairments or developmental disabilities. The group may include both children and adults, and they will all, no doubt, have various expectations about what constitutes a great museum tour. Nevertheless, it is your job to create an environment for sharing.

One of our experienced educators who facilitates museum tours for both youth and adult visitors confided her strategy for ensuring participation. "If you want the tour to be participatory, you need to get the group talking as soon as you meet them."[5] She asks them their first name, where they are visiting from, and if this is their first time at the museum. This begins to "prime" them for the expectation that they will be contributing as the tour continues. The way you respond in these initial encounters may determine the success of your tour. Are you genuinely interested in the answers? Are you welcoming, responsive, and friendly? Consciously or not, the participants are "testing the waters" and deciding whether or not this is really a safe place for them to express their ideas.

Cognitive psychologist Abigail Housen, who has studied and written extensively about museum learning, sums up her vision of what an ideal museum environment would be. "I want people to

Figure 4.1 Participants who are seated comfortably on gallery stools are more likely to sustain conversations in front of works of art than those who are that are standing.
FILIP WOLAK

feel that they can respond to a work of art in their own voice. I want them to feel excitement from asking their own questions and engaged as they discover their own answers. Being present in that way in front of a work of art is the beginning of forming a personal relation with a work of art, an intimacy which will enliven the viewer and can grow with the viewer, not ahead of the viewer."[6]

There is a good amount of neurological evidence that supports the idea that people who do not feel comfortable cannot learn. Feelings like embarrassment, boredom, or frustration can block the ability to make the necessary brain connections for learning to take place. Participants need reassurance that all responses to gallery activities are welcomed, valued, and respected. Participating in a gallery activity is not about who creates the most proficient drawing, the most elegant poem, or most graceful pose. It is about doing and learning and appreciating the unique contributions of everyone in the group. Once you have considered the emotional comfort of your group, it is time to consider their physical comfort.

Provide Physical Comfort

The difference between whether your group can fully participate, or not, may be the option to sit down. For all adult audiences it is important to have somewhere to sit. When I am traveling to another museum to give a workshop, my first question is usually, "Do you have gallery stools?" Gallery stools are the number-one tool of the gallery educator who wants to incorporate activities into their tours. Adults cannot comfortably look, converse, write, or share when they are standing up. A standing tour can be likened to a cocktail party; a tour with the option to sit down as dinner around the family table. These are two very different experiences.

Younger visitors like camp and school groups can sit on the floor in front of the works of art. It is thoughtful to provide their teachers and chaperones with gallery stools. For families and inter-generational groups, we may use cushions on the floor, with gallery stools available as an option.

Some teen groups will sit on the floor, but some will grumble about being treated as kids. I have also seen this result in them lying all over each other. Provide gallery stools if you can. This will greatly enhance their attention and behavior, and it will treat them as the young adults that they are.

I suggest that you have a gallery stool for yourself as well. Although many museum educators have their group seated while they stand, I much prefer to sit down with the group, not because I don't have the energy to stand while facilitating, but because being on the same physical level conveys the message that I am part of this learning community.

If your museum already has gallery stools—great. If you need to purchase them, you will find that the selection quite limited. The criteria for gallery stools should be this: (1) sturdiness, (2) portability (lightweight/easily carried), (3) easily stored but accessible, (4) cost-effective, and (5) aesthetically pleasing. Locating and purchasing gallery stools is a topic that frequently shows up on AAM's *Museum Junction Open Forum Digest,*[7] an online community for the museum field that allows you to share your expertise, knowledge, and experiences to help others resolve challenges. Periodic posts suggest that museums across the nation are looking for the perfect gallery stool that meets all of these specifications.

Hint: if you cannot find anything that meets your criteria when searching "gallery stools," try "camping stools" or even surgical supply products. As a side note, if anyone reading this book who is looking to start a new business, the field of museum education could use some new and affordable options for gallery stools!

The use of gallery stools can greatly diminish a phenomenon known as *museum fatigue*, the time when a museum visitor begins to feel mental/physical exhaustion, a condition first described in a 1916 study,[8] that has since received widespread attention in popular and scientific contexts. One remedy to this more-than-century-long concern is distributing gallery stools on your tours. Visitors who experience their first tour using gallery stools after years of only being upright in museums have said to me, "I could concentrate on the art for the first time! Usually I am so aware of my aching feet and back that I can't give the art my full attention."[9]

With the emotional and physical needs of your group met, we can now consider the guidelines for creating gallery activities.

Help to Meet Tour/Lesson Goals

An activity should always be purposeful. How will this activity contribute to meeting goals for the gallery or classroom experience? In short, why are we doing this? Think about what the activity will accomplish and how it enhances connections with the work of art. Some possibilities include observing the work more closely, exploring a technique, promoting a better understanding process, and materials or activating prior knowledge. Be aware of why and how the activity supports your teaching goals.

Relate Directly to a Work of Art and Deepens Understanding of that Work

The gallery activity should be designed to deepen the connection with the work of art you are focusing on. It should encourage the viewer to look at, think about, or respond to the work and enhance their understanding and/or connection to it.

Use Only Gallery-Safe Materials

In many museums, gallery-safe materials are often limited to pencils, colored pencils, and paper, but consider novel ways to use these materials. For writing or drawing activities, provide visitors with a hard backing like Masonite or heavy cardboard. Different museums have different parameters for materials that are allowed in the galleries. For instance, we were surprised and delighted to learn that Model Magic®[10] was deemed a safe material for gallery use at the Guggenheim by our curatorial and conservation staff.

We cannot use glue, glue sticks, or scissors in the galleries, but that doesn't prevent us from doing collage activities. Precut papers can be arranged on cardstock and adhered by covering with a clear plastic laminating sheet.[11] Other gallery-safe materials will be discussed in subsequent chapters.

Have Simple, Understandable Directions

If the directions for an activity are too complicated, it will not work. The best activities are almost intuitive. The participants understand what you are asking them to do, because the activity flows naturally from the work of art being observed. Too many times I have heard museum educators give elaborate instructions and watched as the group of participants looked entirely baffled about what they were supposed to do next. Keep the instructions simple!

For groups with special needs, this is even more important. Give directions in simple, understandable steps. Consider providing directions in more than one modality: say it, write it, then check for understanding.

Consider Interpersonal Dynamics

Activities can be structured as whole group interactions or as smaller working groups, with a partner or individually. With a bit of planning and thought, many activities can be structured and facilitated to support one or more of these dynamics. The educator should consider *why* they might prefer to introduce one structure over another. Sometimes these decisions are made on the spot out of necessity.

As an example, when I was doing a workshop for art teachers in Singapore, I asked participants to share some of the writing they had done in response to looking at an artwork. Dead silence prevailed. I wondered why a strategy that usually worked well was now "tanking." Then I asked them to turn to a neighbor and share their writing. An instant buzz of sharing and learning began to pervade the room. With that small tweak, an unsuccessful activity was transformed into one that worked.

What I had failed to consider were cultural differences between the United States and Singapore, where people are less comfortable speaking publicly than in the United States. The moment I changed "public space" (speaking to the whole group) into "private space" (speaking to a single person sitting next to you), the environment and safety factor was changed and supported the sharing of ideas.

Are Developmentally Appropriate

Many of the activities described in this book can be used across ages, but it is imperative to consider developmental differences when you plan your activities. A fourth grader may love taking the pose of a ballerina pictured in an Edgar Degas painting, but if you ask a sixteen-year old to do the same activity, the result may be utter humiliation.

When planning an activity for a particular age group, Chip Wood's book, *Yardsticks: Children in the Classroom Ages 4–14*,[12] can be enormously helpful in describing the physical, social, emotional, and cognitive characteristics at each stage of development.

I have heard people recount museum experiences that made them reluctant to ever visit another museum again. Your motto should be the same as a physician's: "Do no harm." Design your activities with your audience in mind. Not all activities are transferable for all audiences.

For groups with special needs, understanding their abilities is at least as important as understanding their limitations. I have seen educators devise many brilliant and yet simple accommodations that allow for participation. *Visual boards* (also called communication boards and touch boards) and/or providing photocopied printouts of the artworks you are focusing on, may allow nonverbal groups to communicate their responses in front of works of art.[13] The use of touch ob-

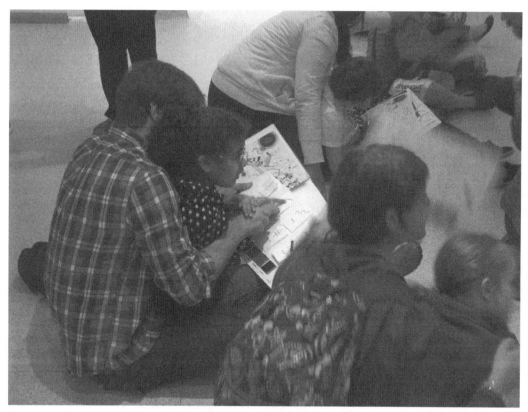

Figure 4.2 Students participating in *Guggenheim for All: Reaching Students on the Autism Spectrum*, use communication boards to share their responses to *Composition 8,* a painting by Vasily Kandinsky.

jects and iPads can enlarge the details of a work of art and help visitors with visual impairments to participate more fully. For visitors with hearing impairments, assistive listening devices amplify sound, particularly speech, and reduce extraneous background noises.[14] The list of possible accommodations begins with learning more about the group before their visit, so that the educator can plan the most effective participatory strategies.

Activities Are Participatory, Inclusive, and Allow for Another Level of Engagement in Addition to Discussion

This is what I love about gallery activities. We do them together. Everyone participates, even the facilitator, because the activity is designed to get everyone in the group involved. If possible, join in on the activity. It gives you something to do besides "hovering" and also provides a realistic estimation of when it's time to wrap up.

Although it is not possible for all activities, I believe it is desirable for the facilitator to also be a participant for several reasons:

- Doing the activity with the group helps you figure out how much time should be devoted to the task.

Figure 4.3 Participant in the museum's *Mind's Eye* program for visitors with vision loss and blindness views contextual photographs related to the exhibition *Maurizio Catalan: All* on an iPad.
PHOTO: ALEX SEEL

- Doing the activity makes you part of the group, not only as a facilitator but as a learner. It signals, "I can learn something from doing this, too."

- Doing the activity inhibits "hovering." Some museum and art educators believe it shows interest and caring to move though the group looking over shoulders while the group is working. As an art student I always found it inhibiting and anxiety producing. I was super aware of where the instructor was—so much so that it overwhelmed my ability to work freely. I vowed that when I became an instructor, I would always let students know that I was available to talk with them about the progress of their work but would not walk around the workspace, showing up over student's shoulders while they were working. I know many art and museum educators love to circulate during a work session and consider this a hallmark of good teaching, but I believe that letting individuals have some time to work out their responses is a more respectful way to support the development of ideas.

Activities Are Multimodal and May Focus on Writing, Movement, Drawing, Sound, or Touch Objects

This is what this book is about. You will find descriptions of many multimodal activities in part II of this book, so I won't elaborate here.

Include Some Sharing and/or Reflection

Once the activity concludes, there should be a way to share the outcomes. The museum educator needs to be sensitive to the group they are working with. Some groups will be eager to share what has been generated by the activity. You can ask for volunteers—usually a willingness to make eye contact will provide a clue to who is ready and willing to share. Pair sharing or turn and talk is a safer and more intimate way of sharing that can be used when you sense the group might be more guarded. It is also fine for participants not to share the outcome of the activity. The museum educator must always keep in mind that the goal of introducing a gallery activity is not to produce a great drawing or outstanding poem but to offer a way to connect more deeply with a work of art. If participants prefer not to share, that's just fine and doesn't mean that learning and new connections have not been made.

Have Been Tried Out in Advance

With new activities, an idea is not enough. It is imperative to try it out. Do it! Ask your friends and/or colleagues to try it out and provide feedback. Frequently, you will be able to troubleshoot, find where you need to make an adjustment, alter a material, or add a direction.

Are Playful and Fun

Not necessarily "ha-ha" fun, although humor certainly can be an important factor, but fun in a creative, exploratory way. Although most of us understand that play is essential for brain development in kids, it is also important for adults. Our society tends to dismiss play for adults. Play is perceived as unproductive, petty, or even a guilty pleasure. But according to Scott G. Eberle, PhD, editor of the *American Journal of Play*, "We don't lose the need for novelty and pleasure as we grow up."[15]

Many gallery activities include elements of play (and fun) that help to fuel imagination, creativity, and problem-solving abilities. Play can support learning, and connect you to others and the world around you.

After participating in a day-long gallery teaching marathon, my colleague Rachel Ropeik mused, "How can I take that spirit of fun, unexpected experiences in the museum and layer it into my job? How can I give the teachers I work with—especially now, when so many are stressed over standards and evaluation—the same kind of joyful, playful invigoration that I felt from all these NAEA sessions and colleagues? How can I spread my own belief that sometimes the most fun you can have in a museum comes from doing something within its walls that you would never have expected to do?"[16]

Support Divergent Outcomes

Just like a well-crafted open-ended question should support multiple interpretations and responses, a well-crafted gallery activity should elicit a diversity of fresh and sometimes even startling insights and ideas. Activities are only successful if they are structured to encourage personal interpretation and solutions. The activity asks the participant to exercise their thinking and creativity. That is the interesting part—how the same directions can elicit such varied responses. Encourage and reinforce these divergent responses.

Require Reflection and Sometimes "Tweaking" by the Educator

The first time you introduce a new activity, you may come away from the experience thinking, "That went great" or "I'll never do that again." Some activities will go well from the start, but if an activity falls flat, take some time to think about where and why it went wrong. Sometimes a very simple "tweak" can be the difference between an unsuccessful and successful activity.

Conclusion

This may seem like a lot of things to think about when creating a gallery activity, but with a bit of practice and experimentation, you will begin to develop a "sixth sense" regarding what will work for which audience. If your activity meets the criteria above, it has a pretty good chance of success.

Part II

Chapter 5

Writing Activities

"I don't know what I think until I write it down." —Joan Didion, author[1]

"I write because I don't know what I think until I read what I say." —Flannery O'Connor, author[2]

"I don't know what I think until I write it, and then I'm always surprised by my thoughts, and kind of ashamed, thrilled and mortified at the same time." —Jerry Saltz, art critic[3]

Writing activities can be as simple as jotting down a single word in response to looking at a work of art, or it can involve longer, more involved pieces of writing, including journal entries, narrative descriptions, character development, dialogues, or poetry.

The importance of writing down a response to the question, "What did you notice about this work?" cannot be overemphasized. Although many museum educators begin their tour stops with this question, it is more typical for the group to begin a conversation by only responding verbally. Then why write?

The process of writing something down is an act of commitment. It is an expression of your individual opinion in direct response to an encounter with a work of art, before those around you voice their ideas and begin to influence and modify your first and direct impressions. It gives participants on your tour a chance to think before the open-ended discussion of the artwork begins. The thought inside your head is now out in the world—committed to paper. Whether or not you decide to voice your ideas to the tour group in the ensuing conversation, you have formed and recorded an independent idea. This skill of taking in stimuli, processing your thoughts about it, and finding ways to clearly express your personal response is vital to all communication.

Following a gallery experience, one of the most frequent comments I hear from participants is that they were surprised by the range of responses to the same artwork. To me it is less surprising. We come to the task of looking at a work of art with different backgrounds, experiences, and areas of expertise, so it should be expected that we will be drawn to different aspects of a single

Figure 5.1 Camille Pissarro (1830–1903)
The Hermitage at Pontoise, ca. 1867
Oil on canvas
59 5/8 x 79 inches (151.4 x 200.6 cm)
SOLOMON R. GUGGENHEIM MUSEUM, NEW YORK, THANNHAUSER COLLECTION, GIFT, JUSTIN K. THANNHAUSER, 1978
78.2514.67

artwork. For instance, when looking together at Camille Pissarro's painting *The Hermitage at Pontoise*, ca. 1867,[4] a landscape depicting life in a French village, different visitors might comment on the weather, the shadows, the gestures of the figures, the composition, or even the cracks on the painting's surface. Beginning the time in front of an artwork with an opportunity to look and write down first impressions increases the chances of getting diverse responses into "the mix."

For some participants, writing down a single word will be an enormous struggle. For others, the words and ideas will flow more freely. Our job as educators is to create an environment where varied ideas can be shared, considered, and debated. One of the big goals of looking together at works of art is getting participants accustomed to digesting their perceptions and expressing their insights in words.

For those educators working with school-aged youth, there is another pragmatic reason for adding writing activities to your art inquiries. At all levels and subject areas, educators are tasked with developing the literacy, language, and writing skills of their students. Like it or not, we live in a world where language arts and mathematics are the privileged subject areas. By regularly asking students to write (and talk) in response to looking at art, you are helping them to develop

Figure 5.2 Some works of art suggest their own activities. Museum educator Jen Brown asks students to complete the sentence suggested by Untitled, 1997, a painting by Christopher Wool.

language skills and to express their ideas. This benefit has been researched and documented in an independent study. In 2003, the Guggenheim's artist in residency program, Learning Through Art, was awarded a major grant from the U.S. Department of Education to examine the impact of its pioneering program on third-grade students' ability to describe and interpret art and to apply these skills to understanding written text. The study, *Teaching Literacy Through Art, 2002–2006*, was conducted in tandem with independent evaluators Randi Korn and Associates. It focused on a sample of over 500 students from four schools in New York City and found that regularly asking students to write and talk about art helps students become better learners, thinkers, and communicators.[5]

Many books have been written by language arts educators focusing on how works of art can be used in the service of developing stronger writing skills. I am flipping the equation. I want language skills used to make stronger connections to works of art. Although regular use of the

Figure 5.3 Student completes the sentence, YOU MAKE ME

techniques outlined below will also support literacy development, the primary goal here is to get participants to express their responses and make deep connections with works of art.

The following writing activities are by no means exhaustive. There are more variations on writing activities than any other form. These are but a few of the myriad possibilities that the act of writing can provide in response to considering a work of art. Some are designed to promote individual writing; others are more collaborative and get participants involved in creating a collective response. Most require only the most rudimentary materials—a pencil, a piece of paper, something to lean on as you write, and the ability to sit down—on the floor for younger audiences, on a gallery stool for adults. Where additional materials are required, they lead off the description. As in all of the suggested activities, I encourage you to try them, modify them to suit your own teaching style, audience, and content, and to invent your own.

Callouts/Thought Bubbles

Materials

Graphic Callouts can be made or purchased. They can be found on Microsoft Word > Insert > Shapes > Callouts.[6] There are also commercially available "sticky notes" that can be ordered online.

This activity is used in conjunction with works that include people or animals. "Callouts" or "thought bubbles" are used in cartoons to indicate what the characters are thinking or saying. This is a good strategy to use with individual or group portraits. Each participant receives a blank

Figure 5.4 Students writing in callouts/thought bubbles in response to the prompt, "What might the person in this painting be saying or thinking?"

"callout." They are then asked to write down what a character might be thinking or saying. The responses are shared with the group.

Variation 1

For works with multiple figures such as city or crowd scenes. Each person in the group silently selects one of the figures in the work and completes their callout. As each callout is read, the group tries to guess who it might be attributed to.

Variation 2

Photocopies of the artwork with superimposed thought bubbles are distributed to the group. They write down what they think each character is saying or thinking and then share out loud.

Concrete Poetry

Materials

Strips of 11" x 17" ledger paper divided into thirds "the long way." Pencils, colored pencils, Prismacolor Art Stix® woodless colored pencils.[7]

Concrete poetry uses the graphic arrangement of letters, words, or symbols to visually convey additional meaning. This activity is a combination of writing and drawing to create a response to a work of art.

Divide the tour group so that you have two or more working groups. Provide strip(s) of paper to each participant. Each participant writes a word or two in response to the work of art. The word is written on the paper in a way that expresses its meaning. All words are placed on the floor. Each group works together, arranging the words into a poem. A representative from each group reads the newly created poem to the other group as they reflect on the work of art. Since there is a visual component to this writing—looking at the way the words are drawn adds additional meaning. This activity is equally effective for students studying poetry or graphic design.

Five Senses Exquisite Corpse

Materials

8.5" x 11" sheets of copy paper cut into thirds "the long way" and then folded into five horizontal sections.

Exquisite corpse is a collaborative writing game that traces its roots to the Parisian Surrealist movement. Exquisite corpse is played by several people, each of whom writes a word or phrase on a sheet of paper, folds the paper to conceal it, and passes it on to the next player for his or her contribution.[8]

This activity is perfect for self-conscious teenagers. They can write their impressions without divulging their identity. Everyone participates anonymously. No single person is responsible for the frequently eloquent results. The hardest part of this activity is teaching the group how to fold the paper so that the final results can be read coherently to the rest of the group.

Everyone focuses on the selected work of art. The educator asks participants to write a word or short phrase in the top section in response to the following directive: Write down something that you *see*. The written response is then folded back so that it cannot be seen as it is passed to the person on the left. (Be sure to review the route in which the papers will be passed in advance.) In the second section, the participant writes down a word in response to the question, "What might you *hear*?" Again, fold back the paper and pass to the left. "What might you *smell*? What odors seem to permeate this work?" Fold back the paper and pass to the left. "What might you *taste*?" Fold back the paper and pass to the left. For the last and bottom section, ask the group to write a word to describe a tactile element. "What might you *feel* or *touch*? What texture is suggested?" Once all five sections and five senses are completed, participants can now unfold the paper, read their collaborative writing, and share with the group.

Character Development

How much can we conjecture about a person we encounter in a portrait? Ask participants to write a character description that answers the following questions:

How old do you think this person is?

What is their mood and how can you tell?

What would make them most happy and most sad?

What might they do when they are not being painted?

Describe their typical day.

What do you think is their favorite meal? Why?

Do you think they have a family? A hobby? A pet? What makes you say that?

Participants should write their responses and support their assumptions with evidence from the work of art. This activity can be followed by a conversation about what information can be accurately deduced from evidence in a painting or photograph and what cannot. You will find many examples of graphic organizers online that are freely available to reproduce and suggest dozens of other questions that can be queried.

Diaries and Journals

After having an open-ended dialogue about a portrait painting, ask participants to imagine the subject of the painting writing in their diary or journal. Write the entry from the first person, as though you became the subject. This strategy is useful in helping participants empathize with subjects that are not contemporary with us.

Daily Schedule

This activity is designed to be used with portraits and helps viewers empathize with the subject and think more deeply about the life of the person portrayed, especially those from bygone eras. I have most frequently used this activity with Pierre-Auguste Renoir's *Woman with Parakeet*, 1871,[9] but it would work well with many portraits and helps the viewer to consider the life of the subject beyond the single moment that we see depicted. At the top of the activity sheet are the words, *Woman with Parakeet's Daily Schedule*. Under that are three sections: (1) Morning, with some lines to fill in her morning activities, then (2)Afternoon, and (3) Evening. It is interesting how this simple activity allows the group to articulate their assumptions and projections about who this person is and how their time is spent.

Writing Dialogue

If you have works of art in your galleries that include two or more figures, break the group into pairs to imagine and write a dialogue between these two characters. Participants should consider not only the content of the conversation but also the type of language and diction that is suggested. When done, have them take on the personas of each character and do a dramatic reading to the group. When participants focus on the same two characters, it is interesting to note whether the resulting writings have similar or very different outcomes.

For a variation of this activity, have the pair of participants stroll through a gallery and choose characters from two different paintings. They should create a dialogue imagining what these two characters might say to one another, and when done, share with the group.

Figure 5.5 Pierre-Auguste Renoir (1841–1919)
Woman with Parakeet, 1871
Oil on canvas
36 1/4 x 25 5/8 inches (92.1 x 65.1 cm)

WOMAN WITH PARAKEET'S

Daily Schedule

MORNING:

_____

_____

_____

_____

AFTERNOON:

_____

_____

_____

_____

EVENING:

_____

_____

_____

_____

Figure 5.6 *Woman with Parakeet's Daily Schedule.*

Collaborative Poetry

Following a discussion of an artwork, divide the tour group into smaller groups of five or six participants who sit in a circle together. Distribute pencils and one index card to each participant. As they look at the work of art, ask each participant to write down one word on the card that they would use to describe the painting. Pass the index card with their word written on it to the person to your left. Use the new word you have just received into a sentence that relates to the artwork. When the sentences are completed, the group works together to decide on the best sequence for the sentences. When done, a representative from each group reads the final collaborative writing to the other group(s).

Figure 5.7 Adult visitors collaborate on a writing activity.
PHOTO: FILIP WOLAK

In a variation of this activity, each participant picks one area of the painting and writes a sentence focusing on that detail. Gather the sentences into a collaborative poem and discuss how well the poem captures the essence of the painting.

Haiku

Haiku is a traditional form of Japanese poetry that consists of just three lines. The first and last lines of a haiku have five syllables. The middle line has seven syllables. The lines rarely rhyme. Because traditional haiku poems are often inspired by nature, I suggest using this responsive activity in connection with works of art that focus on natural themes. Many graphic organizers that help with structuring the syllables of a haiku are available online and freely available for download.

Cinquains

Another quick writing activity that will provide a "snapshot" reaction to a work of art is the creation of a cinquain; short poems consisting of five, usually unrhymed lines containing, respectively, two, four, six, eight, and two syllables.[10] Cinquains are somewhat easier to create than haikus. Many graphic organizers are available online and are freely available to reproduce.

Line #1: Title of work of art

Line #2: Two describing words

Line #3: Three words expressing an action

Line #4: Four feeling words

Line # 5 What you would name the work of art

Before and After

Look closely at the featured work of art and write down what might happen before or after this moment. This activity can also be facilitated by drawing or acting out the changes.

Getting Inside

Ask participants to imagine they are traveling into the painting. Visually explore the environment you have entered and eventually "land" and settle into a specific place inside this painted world. Such an involvement invites participants to "climb" inside the painting or sculpture.[11] Write a description of how things appear from this new vantage point.

Untitled No More

Many modern and contemporary artists have chosen not to provide titles for their works. On the Guggenheim's website alone, dozens of the works are *Untitled*. Conduct a discussion focusing on one or more works that are untitled. Why would an artist decide not to provide a title for their work? Then ask participants to write what they think would be an apt title. Share the responses and discuss what aspects of the work they used to inspire their title.

Leading with a Title

We are accustomed to looking at a work of art and its accompanying object label almost simultaneously. In most museums, "object labels" are positioned in close proximity to the artwork, and many visitors consult the label even before considering the art. For some works, however, the title the artist has assigned to their work goes against expectations. This can be the basis for interesting discussions.

As an example, before looking at the work, I tell participants we are about to see a work of art by the artist Constantin Brancusi titled *Little French Girl*[12] and give them a few minutes to write down what they think this work might look like. We then look together at the work and discuss how the reality of the work is similar or different from their expectations. There are endless examples of works that can be used for this activity.

Whip-Around

This activity combines writing with discussion and encourages both close observation and the development of listening skills. Have participants comfortably seated in front of a work of art. Provide each with paper and pencil. Give them five minutes to write down all the things they notice about the artwork. The list should be as long and inclusive as possible. Then begin going around the group in order with each person contributing a new item from his or her list. If someone else mentions something on your list first, you must cross it off. See how many times you can go around the group without repeating any comments. At the conclusion of this activity, discuss the experience. Participants are frequently surprised how this activity made them aware of things they might have missed if not looking together with others. This activity

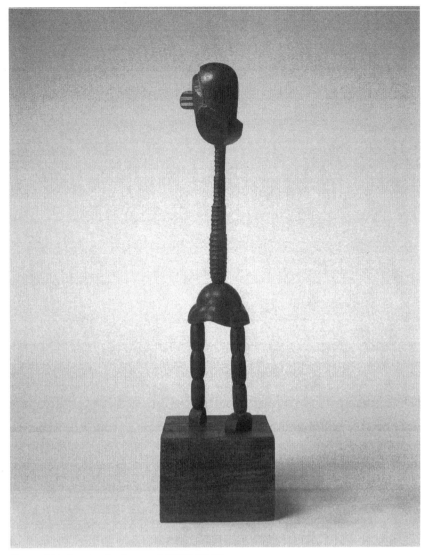

Figure 5.8 Constantin Brancusi (1876–1957)
Little French Girl (The First Step [III]), ca. 1914–1918 (mounted by museum, 1953)
Oak on pine base
figure: 49 x 9 3/8 x 9 1/4 inches (124.5 x 23.8 x 23.5 cm); base: 11 x 15 1/4 x 13
inches (27.9 x 38.7 x 33 cm)
SOLOMON R. GUGGENHEIM MUSEUM, NEW YORK, GIFT, ESTATE OF KATHERINE S. DREIER, 1953
53.1332
© 2017 ARTISTS RIGHTS SOCIETY (ARS), NEW YORK/ADAGP, PARIS

also requires that participants listen carefully to each other so that they do not repeat the same observation.

To emphasize how much there is to notice in a single work of art, a master list can be created on a sheet of poster paper.[13]

See-Think-Wonder

Project Zero in the Harvard Graduate School of Education was formed in 1967 to conduct research on learning and assessment in and through the arts.[14] One set of strategies that has emerged from their research is visible thinking, "a flexible and systematic research-based approach to integrating the development of students' thinking with content learning across subject matters."[15] Several of these strategies are highly applicable to gallery teaching and both support the development of thinking skills and deepen content learning. They are short, easy-to-learn mini-strategies that extend and expand students' thinking. One of the protocols is See-Think-Wonder and can be used "for exploring works of art and other interesting things."[16]

During the "See" phase, participants make observations about a work of art. Next, they are asked what they "Think" might be going on in the work. Encourage them to back up their interpretation with reasons. Lastly, the group is asked what they are now wondering based on what they have observed and thought. Try the "I see . . . , I think . . . , I wonder . . . ." routine individually on paper before sharing out as a group. Responses can be written down and recorded so that a group chart of observations, interpretations, and wonderings are listed for all to see.[17] Many See-Think-Wonder graphic organizers are available online and are freely available to reproduce.

This routine closely parallels strategies that many museum educators use. It is common that an inquiry in front of a work of art will begin by asking participants what they notice (see), how they interpret the work (think), and finally what questions they have (wonder).

I Used to Think . . . , Now I Think . . .

"I Used to Think . . . , Now I Think . . . ," is another protocol based on the Project Zero visible thinking routine that helps visitors reflect on how and why their thinking has changed.[18] It can be useful in consolidating new learning and identify new understandings, opinions, and beliefs. It can be used whenever initial thoughts, opinions, or beliefs are likely to have changed as a result of instruction or experience. Although there are many ways to apply this routine, at the Guggenheim we frequently use it as a way for visitors to reflect on their museum experience.

For example: "When you knew you were going to be visiting the museum, you may have had some expectations about what you would experience. Now that you have visited, take some time to think back and then write down your response to the prompt, 'I used to think . . .'

"Now, consider today's experience at the Guggenheim and in a few sentences write down what you currently think about your museum visit. Start your sentences with, 'Now, I think . . .'"

Compare and discuss the responses. This strategy can be applied whenever learners' initial thoughts, opinions, or beliefs are likely to have changed as a result of instruction or experience; for instance, when participants have spent time with unconventional works of art that may initially seem strange or even incomprehensible.[19] As the group becomes more familiar with the art and artist, their ideas may (or may not) change from their initial response to the conclusion of the museum experience. This routine can also be useful in getting participant feedback about courses, workshops, and professional development programs.

Compare and Contrast

It is an innate human trait to be aware of similarities and differences. This trait can be effectively channeled by comparing and contrasting to show connections and disparities between the works you have selected on your tour route. Before beginning, clarify for participants that when *comparing* you will look for things that are similar in both of the works we have looked at. When we are *contrasting*, you will look for aspects of the two works that are different from one another. If the works of art are not hanging side by side in the galleries, I have a small photocopied reproduction available to remind the group of the work we looked at previously.

I provide a sheet of paper to each participant and ask them to fold it in half. On the left side of the paper list all the similarities they notice; on the right, all the differences. After a few minutes we begin discussing their findings. Alternative graphic organizers including Venn diagrams are available online. The success of this activity depends on choosing works carefully.

Manifestos

A manifesto is a written statement that publicly declares the ideals or intentions of its author(s).[20] One of the most famous examples is *The Communist Manifesto* by Karl Marx and Friedrich Engels. During the early twentieth century, almost every new art movement, including the Cubist, Dadaist, and the Surrealist, had a manifesto stating its goals. One of the most strident art manifestos was "The Founding and Manifesto of Futurism," written in 1909 by F. T. Marinetti.[21] It contains some bold, and by today's standards, highly questionable statements.

> "We intend to sing to the love of danger, the habit of energy and fearlessness."

> "We intend to glorify war—the only hygiene of the world—militarism, patriotism, the destructive gesture of anarchists, beautiful ideas worth dying for, and contempt for woman."

> "We intend to destroy museums, libraries, academies of every sort, and to fight against moralism, feminism, and every utilitarian or opportunistic cowardice."

After viewing and discussing a Futurist work of art, I distribute excerpts from the Futurist manifesto and ask participants to identify statements in the manifesto that are confirmed in the artwork. The writing activity may be to add another line to the manifesto that reflects an aspect of the work we are considering, or I might ask participants to write down a goal that they believe art should have. The most ambitious outcome is to begin writing a personal manifesto, a statement of individual beliefs. These statements may be kept confidential or proclaimed to the rest of the group.[22]

First Impressions/Considered Impressions

This activity is especially good for contemporary works that may not initially yield meaning. Give each participant two index cards. At the beginning of the art inquiry, ask each participant to write down a word that comes to mind when they first look at the work of art. After discussing the work, again have them write a word that comes to mind in response to the work. Divide the group into subgroups each with five or six participants. They should then work together to create a poem in response to the artwork that incorporates all the *before* and *after* words that have been generated. Another variation is to create separate *before* and *after* poems to discover how perceptions change as participants become more familiar with the work of art. Participants share the writing they have jointly created with the other groups.

Postcards Home

Materials: Cardstock cut into 4" x 6" rectangles to simulate the size of a postcard. Postcards sold in your museum store may also be used. Although commercially printed postcards may be too expensive for routine distribution, you can make color copies to use with your tour groups.

When I was a kid, when you went away on vacation, you would send a postcard home with a photo of the place on one side, and your writing—recounting the sights you have seen and the new experiences you are having—on the flip side. That custom has largely been supplanted by emails, text messages, and Instagram posts, but you can revive the tradition. In front of any work that depicts a place—ask students to imagine that they are visiting this new environment. Ask them to write home to a friend or family member describing this new place in detail. What experiences have they had? What people they have met?

Postcard Reflections

Another way to reflect on a museum visit is to distribute postcards that have an image of your institution on the back. Toward the end of the tour, ask each participant to write about their museum experience and what was most memorable. Then have them select a recipient and add their address. When done, ask volunteers to share their writing and why they chose that particular person to send their postcard to. If you have the budget, offer to mail these; it makes for a special farewell gift to the group and the person who will receive it.

Verbal Description

We have often heard the phrase, "A picture is worth a thousand words." Verbal description is a way of using words to represent the visual world. This approach to description enables people who are blind or visually impaired to form a mental image of what they cannot see. These detailed descriptions can also be illuminating for the writer who tries to convey the visual complexity of a work of art through words alone and for the viewer who may be directed to look at aspects of a work that would otherwise go unnoticed. Although museum staff members who write verbal descriptions for blind and visually impaired audiences are highly trained and experienced professionals, it can also be used as a rigorous writing exercise—using language to describe a work of art so fully that a mental image of the work can be formed.[23] This is a sophisticated activity that can be used to support the development of descriptive language. A way to facilitate in the galleries might be to first outline the guidelines for writing verbal description on the *Art Beyond Sight* website. Then each participant selects a work and writes a description. This does take time, so only try this with groups that have ample time and interest. When the group reassembles, the writings can be shared. It is best to listen to these with your eyes closed so that you can form the image in your mind's eye. Once participants have heard the verbal description, they will be very interested in locating these works in the galleries and comparing their visualization with the actual work of art. These comparisons will prompt additional discussions.

The organization Art Beyond Sight provides guidelines for people seeking to develop this skill. You can also find examples of verbal descriptions of Guggenheim works at https://www.guggenheim.org/news/verbal-description-audio-tour-now-available-online.

Conclusion

I could go on. There are innumerable writing activities and ways to customize them for your particular audience and the works of art you are considering. You will probably find a few favorites that fit your style and way of teaching. I certainly have my "go to" writing activities that I return to again and again, but don't be afraid to try out new ones and invent your own variations and adaptations.

Chapter 6

Drawing Activities

"You will find yourself becoming fascinated with the wondrous complexity of the thing you are seeing, and you will feel that you could go deeper and deeper into the complexity. Allow this to happen. You have nothing to fear or be uneasy about. Your drawing will be a beautiful record of your deep perception."[1]

"The impulse to draw is as natural as the impulse to talk."[2]

For several years I taught drawing at the college level. We spent the semester developing sensitivity to line, paying attention to how light was distributed across objects, and how a page can be composed to direct the viewer's attention. We began the semester learning to coordinate the movement of our eyes and hand by practicing blind contour drawing. Later we explored how the movement of the figure can be expressed through gesture drawing and then moved on to modeling forms in space. But when I introduce a drawing activity to museum visitors, I don't care about any of that.

My goal in introducing drawing as a museum activity is usually to slow down looking. Drawing demands that we pay attention, look carefully, and slow down our eyes, mind, and body. Although I have taught the various approaches to drawing—contour, gesture, modeling—I only introduce these approaches in the museum environment if I am trying to call attention to a particular aspect of a work of art. For instance, I might introduce contour drawing to better appreciate works with conspicuous lines and edges, gesture drawing for works that suggest movement, or modeling techniques as a way to capture weight and form. However, I am not teaching drawing (any more than I am teaching writing when I introduce writing activities). Instead, I am employing a strategy that will allow visitors to contemplate works of art and architecture in a more concentrated way.

Drawing is completely natural to kids. At the Guggenheim, families can borrow drawing materials, and I am always delighted when I come across kids lying down on our terrazzo floors looking intently at a painting or sculpture and drawing their impressions. It is the simplest, and perhaps most appropriate, interactive strategy for kids. Unfortunately, as kids get older, they start to get self-conscious—not just about drawing, but about everything.

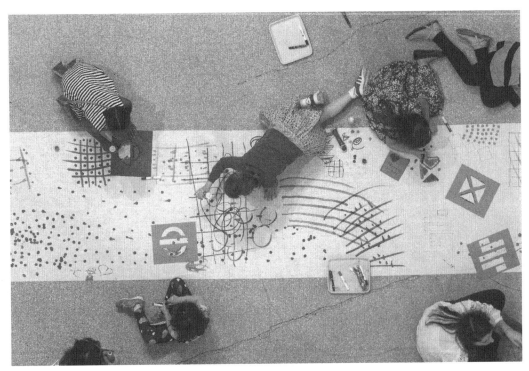

Figure 6.1 Collaborative abstract drawing emphasizing varied mark-making.

Many years ago, as an art education student, I was instructed that younger children should not draw from observation. It was believed that it would stunt their imaginations and be detrimental to their further artistic development. My observation is to the contrary. In her book, Nancy Smith addresses this misconception. She notes that "children are encouraged to use observation drawing to record information in science and social studies, but not in art."[3] In addition to drawing from memory and imagination, observational drawing can be successfully employed with younger children.

Adults come to the museum with various levels of comfort with their drawing abilities. Some will relish the opportunity to draw, but many will immediately apologize for their perceived lack of drawing ability. I frequently hear, "I can't draw a straight line with a ruler." Unfortunately, somewhere during the course of our educational experiences, we come to either think of ourselves as someone who can draw or someone who is "drawing challenged." Many stop drawing after childhood because they feel their attempts at drawing look childish. Basic drawing competence and comfort should be a universal skill that we all develop, but unfortunately in many instances, that is not the case.

Adults who are "drawing insecure" need to be reassured that they will not be required to share or display their drawings unless they want to. Their drawings are records of their careful looking. Like an electrocardiogram records your heart rate, drawings record the act of perception. The goal of a drawing activity is not to make a great drawing, but rather to make great observations. At the conclusion of a drawing activity, the question to ask is "What did you learn?" "What did you see that you had not noticed before?"

Figure 6.2 Paul Cézanne (1839–1906)
Still Life: Plate of Peaches, 1879–1880
Oil on canvas
23 1/2 x 28 7/8 inches (59.7 x 73.3 cm)
SOLOMON R. GUGGENHEIM MUSEUM, NEW YORK, THANNHAUSER COLLECTION, GIFT, JUSTIN K. THANNHAUSER, 1978
78.2514.4

In my earlier life as an art educator, I would only ask students to draw from three-dimensional works. It seemed to me that drawing from two-dimensional works would not be useful, since the artist had already done the hard work by converting a three-dimensional vision of the world onto a two-dimensional surface. I have revised my thinking. Drawing from two-dimensional works of art can help us to see and understand things that would go unnoticed without this form of concentrated looking and recording.

I have had my own revelations while drawing in the galleries. I vividly recall my colleague Rika Burnham[4] facilitating a discussion focusing on Paul Cézanne's (1839–1906) *Still Life: Plate of Peaches* 1879–1880.[5] At first glance, you might see this as a fairly typical still life depicting a bowl of fruit sitting atop a white tablecloth. We were asked to take some time to draw the work and annotate our drawing by writing our observations and perceptions in the margins. The more I looked and drew, the stranger the painting became. I noticed that the peaches were painted more like billiard balls than fruit. If you tried to bite into one of them, you would risk serious injury. As I drew the tablecloth, I realized that there was no table supporting the fabric. The two pieces of fruit were literally defying gravity, somehow levitating rather than crashing to the floor. The background of the painting also held mysteries. The wallpaper refused to stay anchored to the background. Parts of it strangely floated to the front of the picture plane. Without drawing this painting, I would have never noticed or appreciated the spatial shifts or plays of illusion that Cézanne included in this work. I have never again looked at that painting or Cézanne's work in the same way.

In order to encourage visitors to draw from works of art (rather than capturing them with their smartphones), the Rijksmuseum in Amsterdam launched #hierteekenen (or "Start Drawing").[6] According to Wim Pijbes, emeritus general director of the Rijksmuseum, "In our busy lives we don't always realize how beautiful something can be. We forget how to look really closely. Drawing helps because you see more when you draw."[7]

For drawing activities, I provide Ebony drawing pencils. They make a dark, rich, responsive line, and look like "art materials" that nonart audiences usually greet with the comment, "What nice pencils!" For drawing activities, a medium-quality drawing paper is used. It has a slightly textured surface that is better for drawing than the slicker paper used in copier machines, but either will work.

Something to remember is to keep the paper relatively small. Although in art school you are always being encouraged to "work big" for many adults, the larger the expanse of blank white paper, the more intimidating it is. The largest paper I use in the galleries is 9"x 12," with most being even smaller. I bring along some pencil sharpeners with receptacles for shavings and erasers: pink pearl, art gum, or soap. For adding color ,we use colored pencils or Prismacolor Art Stix® that are marketed as "woodless colored pencils."[8] You will also need a hard-surface Masonite or thick cardboard for a good drawing surface. We stock a supply of oversized drawing boards.[9] Their main advantage is to make the user feel validated: "Look at my big drawing board." Although younger visitors will be comfortable sitting or lying on the floor as they draw, adult audiences will need some sort of seating, so that their bodies are comfortable enough to concentrate on drawing.[10]

Figure 6.3 A padded cushion offers comfort for this brother and sister, while a piece of heavy cardboard provides a firm drawing surface.

Drawing from observation is a frequent and time-honored activity in the galleries of art museums, but it is not the only way to approach drawing. The process of drawing can also be used as a problem-solving activity, to spur imagination, to diagram ideas and concepts, recall memories, and understand abstraction. Drawing activities can be used to encourage close looking, to imagine, to reflect, and to communicate. I have therefore divided these drawing activities into two categories: those that focus on observation and those that are more conceptual and call upon imagination and memory.

As with all gallery activities, be clear on your teaching goal when selecting a particular drawing activity to pair with a specific work of art. Is your goal to encourage careful observation, to capture movement, grasp structure, or record details? These are just a few of the possible reasons for adding a drawing activity to your tour.

Figure 6.4 Family tour participants imagine and draw what this Mario Merz (1925–2003) sculpture might contain.

Drawing from Observation

Drawing from Sculpture—Multiple Views

Sculpture "in the round" demands that it be considered from various angles. In approaching these works, I begin by asking the group to slowly walk around the sculpture. Distribute 9"x 24" pieces of paper that have been folded into four sections. (Cut 18" x 24" paper in half "the long way," then fold it in half and in half again). These papers should then be folded "accordion style." This ensures that all of the drawings will wind up on the same side of the paper so that the results can be viewed as a progression. Of course, for vertically oriented works it is best to hold the paper vertically; for horizontal works—horizontally. You may need to adjust the size of the paper for works with less traditional proportions.

Figure 6.5 Family tour participants draw from sculptures by Lee Ufan (b. 1936).
PHOTO: VIRGINIA HOFFMAN

Participants are seated on gallery stools in a circle around the sculpture. They will draw this work from four points of view. In the first drawing paper "compartment," take a few minutes to draw the work from your current vantage point. After a few minutes of drawing, participants move to a gallery stool one-quarter of the way around the sculpture. Draw from that vantage point. Then they move halfway around the work and finally from three-quarters way around the work so that participants have drawn it from all four sides, with one drawing in each of the four folded compartments. Assuming you have twelve participants, you would move three seats each time; with twenty participants on your tour, you move five seats. When the rotation is complete, talk about what you saw, learned, and discovered.

Annotated Drawings

After discussing the work of art, distribute sheets of 9"x 12" drawing paper, a drawing surface/backing, and pencils. Ask participants to draw the approximate proportional format of the work

Figure 6.6 A participant creates an annotated drawing that combines drawing and writing.

of art on their paper leaving a wide margin so that they have room to make notes. Create a diagram of the work inside the format. It is fine to spend more time on the areas of the work that attracted your attention. In the margins around the drawing, make notations about things you noticed, discovered, and so forth. The group then shares their "findings."

Viewfinders

If you look online for a definition of *a viewfinder* you will find, "a device on a camera for showing the area of the subject to be included in the picture."[11] Yes, but a viewfinder need not be on a camera. It can simply be a way to put a frame around any anything you are looking at. Why would you want to do that? The use of a viewfinder can help to focus attention on an area of a work of art. It works best with works that are complicated, include details, and are difficult to fully absorb in a single view.

I use 35mm slide mounts as viewfinders. Before PowerPoint became ubiquitous, art history was taught with 35mm slides. The empty slide mounts with their 1"x 1.5" rectangular "cutout" make perfect viewfinders. They are durable—usually made from plastic and a single box can last your whole career, providing you remember to collect them at the end of the tour. They can still be purchased online,[12] but you can also make viewfinders by cutting a 1"x 1.5" rectangle into the center of an index card. I have also made square and circular viewfinders from segments of paper towel or toilet paper rolls.

After discussing the work of art, distribute the viewfinders. It is important that participants understand that what they see through the viewfinder *is* what they will draw. It is also important that they understand that the shape of the viewfinder *is* the shape of their drawing—so either provide a drawing surface that is proportional to the viewfinder (if you are using a standard slide mount

Figure 6.7 Using 35mm slide mounts as viewfinders to focus on details in a painting.

some options might be a paper cut to 4"x 6" or 8"x 12") or have participants draw a proportional rectangle on their paper. Oh, if you are holding your viewfinder horizontally—your drawing format is a horizontal rectangle. If you are holding your viewfinder vertically, your drawing format is a vertical rectangle. It wouldn't even occur to me to mention this except that I have seen participants holding the viewfinder horizontally, while drawing holding their paper vertically.

Once each participant has a viewfinder, have them experiment with looking through them. What happens when they hold the viewfinder close to their eye and focus on the work of art? What happens when they hold the viewfinder with their arm fully extended? This is your manual "zoom in," "zoom out" feature. Have them scan the work of art through the viewfinder and find an area that is of interest. Once they settle on an area, you need to hold the viewfinder steady and draw everything you see through it on the paper. It may be useful to close one eye.

When I taught drawing, I would give this assignment asking students to take their viewfinder outside and frame an interesting patch of grass to draw. Now I use this device to frame interesting segments of art.

Once the drawings are complete—or at least in substantial progress, ask participants to discuss what they saw and learned.

Modeled Drawing

After discussing a sculptural work—best with works in stone or marble—provide pieces of medium gray paper and a black-and-white pencil. Ask participants to draw the work using the white pencil whenever the work is convex or moves toward them. Use the black pencil wherever the sculpture recedes. Participants are sometimes quite surprised at how this technique provides a sense of dimensionality.

Drawing from Architecture

I realize that the Guggenheim's Frank Lloyd Wright architecture is unique. We consider the building to be the most important object in our collection, and according to Google, the Guggenheim is the most photographed building in the world.[13] This led me to design a recurring program titled Drawing the Guggenheim. It is a very simple workshop. I show historical photographs focusing on the history and construction of the museum, facilitate a short architectural tour, and then send the participants out into the museum with drawing materials and gallery stools to draw for an hour from a favorite vantage point and then discuss what they discovered.

When people think about the Guggenheim, they envision a smooth spiral ramp, but in reality, the museum's architecture is surprisingly complex and eccentric. The best and maybe only way to discover and experience this is through drawing. The other benefit of developing this workshop is that it is "evergreen." I can offer it during installation, on Wright's birthday, or in conjunction an annual New York City–wide celebration of architecture known as Archtober. It is also appropriate for a wide range of audiences. I have had professional architects and an aunt with her eight-year-old nephew in the same workshop. I am including this suggestion since I know that

Figure 6.8 Visitors are invited to draw the museum's architecture and post their drawings in the museum and on social media.
PHOTO: EU JIN JEONG

the Guggenheim is not the only museum with an architecturally significant building. More and more museums are not only designed to exhibit art, but are in themselves visually compelling and/or historically significant.

Consider focusing visitors not only on the artworks hung on the walls, but also on the container that houses the art. This focus allows for a truly multigenerational program that can be as relevant for an eight-year-old as it is for a professional architect.

Every building has a story and this focus can be a motivation for finding out more about your local public school, place of worship, or neighborhood landmark.

Drawing from Imagination

Exquisite Corpse

Exquisite corpse is a collaborative drawing or writing game that traces its roots to the Parisian Surrealist Movement of the 1920s. The name was dubbed by the Surrealist André Breton, who used this technique to disrupt habitual thought processes. Exquisite corpse is played by several people, each of whom draws a section of a figure, folds the paper to conceal it, and passes it on to the next player, who adds another portion of the drawing.[14] This activity is most appropriately used with Surrealist works of art.

Each person begins with a 4.5" x 12" piece of drawing paper (a 9" x 12" sheet that has been cut in half the long way) and folded across into four equal sections. In the top section, each participant draws a head and neck. This can be human, animal, monster, mechanical, alien, and so forth. When the top section is complete, fold it back, letting only the bottom of the neck show. Pass the drawing to the left. In the second section everyone draws the torso and arms, using the neck lines as the starting point. Again, fold that section of the paper back to conceal your drawing, letting just the bottom of the waist line show. Pass the drawing to the person to your left. In the third compartment, draw the figure from the waist to the knees. Fold the paper back and pass to the left. In the last space complete the drawings by adding knees, lower legs, and feet. If you are working with younger children, you may want to simplify the process by having them use last two sections to draw the figure from the waist to the feet. Then each person unfolds the piece of paper they are holding to reveal the collaborative drawing of the figure that has been created. Share the finished drawings and discuss the process of creation.

Emotional Lines

When we look at a work of art, we may have an emotional response. Just like the musical composer can use melody, tempo, and rhythm to trigger emotions, the visual artist uses color, line, rhythm, composition, and so forth to provoke an emotional response, but we don't usually think about "line" as a shared language. It takes some time and thought to understand that lines can be used as a visual vocabulary as eloquently as words or musical notes to evoke feelings. I use this activity before looking at works of art to sensitize participants about how we can literally "read" the emotion of a line.

Have participants fold a sheet of 9"x 12" paper in half crosswise and then in half lengthwise. They should now have four equally sized rectangular compartments the same proportions as the paper. They will also need a pencil and drawing support.

Ask them to choose any one of the compartments and fill it with "angry" lines. "I want you to feel the anger in the center of your body and let those very angry lines fill that space." Allow about thirty seconds for making angry lines. Any longer and the paper will probably be ripped to shreds. Select another compartment. Fill this one with "lazy" lines. What do lazy lines look like? Again, give the group a minute to draw, but their lines may be so lazy they hardly get very far. Fill the next space with lines of "surprise." What do surprised lines look like? Finally, in the last space spend time drawing "confused" lines. Of course, you can substitute other emotions that resonate with the work(s) of art you are considering, and/or you can use a larger paper, with more compartments, and explore how to visually convey other emotions.

Tip: As the facilitator, it is important to bring your own emotions when you introduce each drawing prompt. The more theatrical you are, the more the group will allow their emotions to manifest in their marks.

Once done, ask participants to lay out all the drawings together on the floor of the gallery. Can they identify the compartment with "angry" lines in the marks of others in the group? What shared characteristics can they identify? Can they locate the lazy lines, surprised lines, and confused lines that others have made? Discuss the qualities of these lines.

Then ask participants to describe the emotional qualities of the lines they encounter in the works of art in your galleries. This activity is particularly well-suited for use with abstract works and can inform and clarify how artists use line as an expressive tool.

Conveying Emotion through Color and Form

The artist Vasily Kandinsky (1866–1944) believed that art should express the inner character of things, not their surface appearance. His work seeks to reveal this essence through shape, line, and color. After discussing a work of nonobjective art, provide each participant with a 4" x 6" sheet of drawing paper and drawing materials that include gallery safe color media (colored pencils or Prismacolor Art Stix). Ask students to create a nonobjective composition to express one of the following words through the use of line, shape, and color only: *frustration, loneliness, contentment,* or *exhaustion.*

Ask participants to share their completed works. What are the similarities and differences in how each word was visually expressed? Are there conclusions that can be drawn about how people respond to certain colors, shapes, and lines?[15]

Beyond the Border

Paste a small reproduction of a work of art in the center of a blank sheet of paper. Be sure to leave a wide border (three inches or more). Extend the featured image via drawing into the border created by the blank page.

A variation of this activity can be done before viewing the work of art. Give each participant the same detail from the work of art you will be discussing. They can place/paste it anywhere on their blank sheet of paper. Leave plenty of blank space for drawing. (Maybe a 3" x 4" detail on a 9" x 12" paper.) Extend the detail to suggest what they expect the rest of the image might contain. Then view the work of art and discuss their previewing conceptions versus their discoveries while looking at the work.

Figure 6.9 Pablo Picasso (1881–1973)
Landscape at Céret, Céret, summer 1911.
Oil on canvas
25 5/8 x 19 3/4 inches (65.1 x 50.3 cm)

Find the Image

Cubism is widely regarded as the most innovative and influential artistic style of the twentieth century. A decisive moment in its development occurred during the summer of 1911, when Georges Braque and Pablo Picasso painted side by side in Céret, a town in southern France, each artist producing paintings that are sometimes virtually impossible to distinguish from those of the other. In many of their paintings produced at this time, it is difficult to identify the subject of the work without referencing the title. Among such works is Picasso's *Accordionist*,[16] a composition that one of its former owners mistook for a landscape because of the inscription "Céret" on the reverse.[17]

In *Landscape at Céret*[18] (1911), a canvas painted that summer, Picasso provides some small clues in a maze of muted angles: the zigzag of a stairway, the arch of a doorway, and the suggestion of a curtained window exist as visual clues that must be pieced together. For this painting, as with all Cubist works, the total image must be "thought" as much as "seen."

For this activity I provide an 8.5"x 11" photocopied reproduction of *Landscape at Céret* for each participant and a sheet of tracing paper or vellum that is overlaid on top of the image. Pencils, colored pencils, and drawing support are also available. My drawing prompt is to "find the landscape at Céret." We draw for about ten minutes, each of us emphasizing the elements in our imagined landscape using the (very) few cues that Picasso has provided. The results are frequently surprising, with each participant emphasizing different elements and connecting them in different ways. This activity can be used with many works of Analytic Cubism.[19]

Mind Mapping

The act of drawing may help us to think through ideas and experiences and provide ways to represent concepts and generate new ideas. In a mind map, as opposed to traditional note taking, color, line, shapes, symbols, and writing are combined to give visible form to ideas or perceptions that might otherwise remain hidden. Mind mapping gives the drawer a chance to externalize their thinking and examine it.

One way to begin a mind map is to start in the middle of a blank page by writing or drawing the idea you want to develop. Then, connect related ideas to the center with lines, and use size, color, and line thickness for emphasis. Mind mapping can be used as a reflection tool, by asking participants to draw a mind map of the experience they have had at the museum. The artist Qiu Zhijie (b. 1969) creates extraordinary mind maps that chart historical events and entire exhibitions.[20] He believes that "all of us have a map in our heads of everything."[21] As an activity to complement his work, I asked participants to create a mind map titled *Yesterday,* creating a visualization of their previous twenty-four hours. When done, we talked about how mind mapping a day in their life was different from creating a log or journal entry.

Drawing before Looking

A few years ago, I had the pleasure of working with the artist and educator Luis Camnitzer to create a teacher's guide for a Guggenheim exhibition of contemporary Latin America art.[22] Camnitzer's approach to using works of art on display in the galleries was nearly opposite from how most museum educators work. He was concerned that if students first see works of art in the galleries and then create their own work, the results will be overly influenced by the "solution" on view. Instead, he recommended *problematizing* the work on view—in other words, having the students tackle the same problem as the artist whose work is on view *before* they see it. Although not always practical, some of the Guggenheim educators have found this approach very successful. Some examples of *problematizing* might be:

- The artist Franz Marc (1880–1916) devoted himself to the representation of animals in nature.[23] What animal would you want to show? What type of environment would you create for it? Once students have created their drawings using colored pencils, they visit the galleries to see Marc's solutions.

- With colored pencils, create a small drawing that includes all of the following things: tall mountains, two horses, a rainbow, several buildings, a graveyard, a bird, and a tree. Then, in the galleries, view Franz Marc's *The Unfortunate Land of Tyrol*, 1913[24] and discuss how your conception is similar or different from Marc's.[25]

- The artist Vasily Kandinsky believed that colors could be used to evoke emotions. Select the emotion you want to impart and use color (lines, shapes, and composition) to convey that feeling. Once the drawings are complete, we would view Kandinsky's solutions.

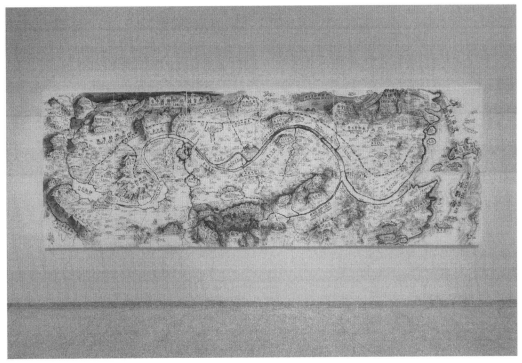

Figure 6.10 Qiu Zhijie b. 1969
Map of the Theater of the World, 2017.
Ink on paper mounted to silk;
six panels, 94 1/2 inches x 23 feet 7 7/16 inches (240 x 720 cm) overall.

There are many advantages to this approach, but it requires additional time and is most successful with groups who are spending extended time at the museum or visiting multiple times. Once students have invested in creating their own work, they are very interested in seeing how the artists on view in the galleries have tackled the same problem.

Chapter 7

Props and Touch Objects

"We do everything so automatically that we have forgotten the poignancy of smell, of physical anguish, of tactile sensations of all kinds." —Lygia Clark[1]

For the most part art museums are "no touch zones." We frequently invoke the phrase "touch with your eyes, not with your hands," but the addition of touch objects and props not only adds a tactile component to tours, but also an element of surprise.

An example may be in order here. One of the better-known works in the Guggenheim's collection is Pablo Picasso's *Woman Ironing*, 1904.[2] This work, from Picasso's "blue period," was done when he first moved to Paris and was a poor, struggling artist living among working-class Parisians. The painting depicts a woman toiling. Her body is elongated and gaunt. Her eyes are darkened orbs. Visitors immediately empathize with her plight. We talk at length about how the artist has portrayed this monument to the struggles of the working class, while still maintaining the humanity and dignity of this individual woman. They notice how the colors, forms, composition, and lines all contribute to the outpouring of emotion that this work evokes. And then from within the bag of materials that I carry with me on all tours, I pull out an iron similar to the one depicted in the painting and pass it around so that each person experiences the mass of the iron. As it passes through the group, I can see surprise and a new understanding on their faces. They are experiencing the heft of the iron. They are imagining what it would be like to endlessly toil with this weight in their hand. I truly feel that no amount of talking can be as powerful as looking at this painting and holding that iron in your hand. This type of visceral learning is equally powerful in the galleries of a museum or in a classroom of a school.

Although museum educators most routinely provide tactile elements for visually impaired visitors, they are appropriate and effective for a variety of audiences. People with developmental or cognitive disabilities may benefit by the introduction of multisensory information. In fact, just about everyone enjoys handling objects that give a sense of textures, weight, and the feel of objects pictured in works of art.

Of course, not every work of art calls for a touch object, but the judicious inclusion of tactile qualities into the gallery tour can enrich and enliven the experience.

Figure 7.1 Pablo Picasso (1881–1973),
Woman Ironing, Paris, 1904.
Oil on canvas,
45 3/4 x 28 3/4 inches (116.2 x 73 cm)

Figure 7.2 Pre-electricity iron is used as a touch object in conjunction with Pablo Picasso's painting *Woman Ironing*, 1904.

Props

If you have works in your collection, especially portraits, that include small items that can be acquired or simulated, they provide opportunities to get more connected to the character pictured, or spirit of the work. In addition to the antique clothes iron mentioned above, some other successful instances of including props include the following:

- A small bird purchased at a craft store is used in conjunction with an exploration of Auguste Renoir's *Woman with Parakeet*, 1871.[3] Holding this simulated bird encourages participants to not only take the pose of Renoir's subject, but also to empathize with the woman depicted and conjecture about her status and emotions.

- A lightweight 11" x 14" picture frame is used with portraits to explore the reading of emotions. Used most effectively with younger visitors, the educator brainstorms a short list of emotions with the group—sad, surprised, confused, angry, and so forth. Each participant then holds the frame in front of their face and expresses an emotion from the list. The group attempts to guess the emotion that is being shown. (See chapter 9, "Drama and Movement Activities," for a more complete description of this activity.)

Figure 7.3 A tour participant uses a prop in the form of a replica of a parakeet to simulate the pose of Pierre-Auguste Renoir's (1841–1919) *Woman with Parakeet,* 1871, that can be seen on the right.

Figure 7.4 Museum educator Jackie Delamatre facilitates a stroller tour and uses a mirror to engage a very young visitor in the theme of portraits.

Figure 7.5 Using a plastic microphone to support interviews and the sharing of family stories.
PHOTO: SCOTT RUDD

- A plastic replica of a microphone enables a child to transform into a "reporter" and ask their parent questions about their immigration experience. Just holding this plastic prop empowers the youth to get information about important family histories.

- Metropolitan Museum of Art educator Nicola Giardina facilitates a discussion of Joan Mitchell's *Sunflower*, 1969.[4] To help us form a visceral connection to Mitchell's abstract depiction, she distributes actual sunflowers to participants and encourages us to explore them through touch and smell. Some of the flowers appear to be fresh and just picked (or purchased); others are dry and in various states of decay. We are asked to compare the qualities of "our flowers" with Mitchell's painting. Examining the flowers and their various colors and texture helps the group to better understand Mitchell's abstract interpretation.

Touch Objects

Many of the works on view in our galleries include the textures and materials of the time when they were created. Providing touchable examples of these materials can enliven your tours and deepen visitor connections.

- For an exhibition of Aztec art, I purchased small samples of turquoise, obsidian, coral, and jade, materials that were used in the works on view. In the galleries tour participants were able to examine these materials. This is especially important when interpreting objects that were designed to be held and used.

Props and Touch Objects

Figure 7.6 Using a few props (notice the small white dog in the painting and on the floor) to take on the persona of the woman in the painting.

- During an exhibition of Russian art, the textures simulated in the eighteenth-century paintings had sumptuous tactile qualities. I was able to get samples of fur (small swatches of ermine donated by a local furrier), brocade, satin, lace, gold braid, and tassels.

- As an extra challenge, I placed each texture sample into a paper bag so that they could be touched, but not seen. Students were asked to put their hand in the bag and try to identify the place in the painting where that texture appeared.

Natural Forms and Close Observation

The works that hang on the walls of many museums demonstrate artists' endeavors to depict the natural world. This process takes enormous focus, care, and empathy. We rarely pay enough attention to the incredible variety of nature and the careful skill of artists who freeze a moment in time.

During an exhibition of Spanish painting, I fell in love with Antonio de Pereda's (1611–1678) painting *Still Life with Walnuts*, 1634, a small oil painting that presents a walnut in various states of "deconstruction."[5] Almost like a stop-motion video we see it whole, then cracked, then opened and ready for consumption. I marveled at the intense observation that this painting reflects, but how could I share this with visitors?

I asked my group to form circles of six or seven participants and then passed around a bag of walnuts, giving everyone a chance to select *their walnut.* "I want you to think of this as your pet walnut. Get to know it in every way you can so that you recognize its special qualities among all the walnuts in the world. Look at it from all angles. Feel its texture. Notice any unique and defining characteristics. Once you know your walnut intimately, pass it to your left and appreciate your neighbor's walnut. How is it similar or different from yours?" Continue passing the walnuts to the left allowing about thirty seconds for each "walnut appreciation" stop. An interesting thing happens when the walnut makes its way back to where it originated. I have seen participants literally clutch their walnut to their heart and exclaim, "This is mine!" In this short time, they have created a bond with their walnut and frequently ask if they can take it home with them. This activity helps me to emphasize nature's variety and the benefits of close observation. Of course, depending on the work you are focusing on, other natural forms can be substituted.

Tools of the Artist

Although many New York City students receive excellent instruction in the arts, I also know that a student can go through their entire K–12 education and never touch a paintbrush. We may assume that our visitors have some prior knowledge about traditional art materials, but I have found that is not always the case. What does a primed and unprimed canvas look and feel like? Canvas stretcher bars? Dry pigments? The surface of a fresco? If we have worked with these materials, we may take for granted their tactile qualities, but having materials that can be handled adds to understanding. We keep samples of fired clay, gold leaf, stone, marble, brass, bronze, aluminum, and steel available as touch objects to accompany tours. Providing touchable examples of the materials that the artist has used to create the work can provide a physical connection as well as contextual knowledge.

Find the Brush

For paintings that contain a wide variety of brushstrokes, I present an array of brushes from small tapered "rounds" suitable for creating delicate lines to broad house painting brushes. For some paintings, additional tools are added. I have recently been carrying around a turkey baster and various wooden sticks similar to those used by Jackson Pollock (1912–1956) to create the web of lines in his drip painting, *Alchemy*, 1947.[6] Participants locate a particular stroke in the painting and then select the type of brush (or other tool) they think might have made it. We also experiment with simulating the way the artist might have held the brush and the gesture that might have produced a particular stroke.

One special brush was provided by the artist Khadim Ali,[7] (b. 1978) who is trained in the tradition of Indian miniature painting. When his work was on view, he gave us a brush that he made using the hair from the back of a cat's neck to use as a touch object.

Figure 7.7 Students experiment with simulating the gesture of the brushstrokes they observe in the painting.

Printmaking Tools

Visitors are particularly vexed about printmaking and what tools and techniques are used to create a print. Depending on the type of print you are focusing on, providing opportunities to examine carving tools, linoleum or wood blocks, brayers, a squeegee or silkscreen, and so forth, can provide learning opportunities.

Contemporary Artists and Materials

Contemporary artists can and do create art from just about anything. They are also frequently more than willing to provide samples of their materials to support visitor experiences.

- Contemporary Cambodian artist, Soheap Pich (b. 1971), provided samples of the rattan he used to create his large-scale sculpture *Morning Glory,* 2011.[8]

- During the retrospective Peter Fischli David Weiss: How to Work Better,[9] we circulated chunks of the polyurethane that the artist duo used to carve their amazing reproductions of everyday objects.

- For an exhibition of Middle Eastern contemporary art, artist Kader Attia (b. 1970) created a scale model of the Algerian town of *Ghardia* from couscous—more than seven hundred pounds of it.[10] Visitors were naturally fascinated by the unusual material. One even tried to taste it. I cooked up some couscous at home adding Attia's other ingredients, wheat paste and salt, and poured the mixture into small plastic cups. After a few days I was able to offer these as touch objects to our curious visitors.

- Artist Rachel Whiteread (b. 1963) works with various casting techniques, making solid form from the hollows of everyday life—the space around a bathtub or inside an empty closet—but when her work *Untitled (Basement)*,[11] a plaster cast of an actual room and basement stairwell was on view at the museum, visitors had a difficult time envisioning the process. By creating some simple plaster casts of a plastic cup, a latex glove, or an iPhone case, I was able to easily demonstrate Whiteread's concept and also provide objects that could be handled.

- For an exhibition of works by the Italian painter Alberto Burri (1915–1995), we secured touch samples of the burlap sacks he used to create his Sacchi/Sacks paintings. The coarse woven material made from jute or sisal was the primary material for Burri's best-known series of works.[12]

Some Thoughts about Smell

Often called "the forgotten sense," a number of behavioral studies have demonstrated what most of us have experienced—that smells can trigger strong emotional memories and induce feelings

Figure 7.8 A visitor explores "Untitled" (Golden), 1995, an installation work by Felix Gónzalez-Torres (1957–1996).

Figure 7.9 Participants in the museum's *Mind's Eye* program for visitors with low vision or blindness, touch clay models replicating works from the exhibition *Maurizio Cattelan: All.*
PHOTO: ALEX SEEL

of "being brought back in time." Researchers have conducted studies suggesting that our sense of smell plays an important role in memory, cognition, and emotion.[13]

For her exhibition at the Guggenheim, Anicka Yi (b. 1971), the 2016 Hugo Boss Prize winner, worked with a team of molecular biologists and forensic chemists to create canisters emitting a scent conceived by the artist.[14] Our museum educators used this opportunity to collect spices, herbs, and flowers, and then use them to discuss scents and memories as part of their tours.

Years ago, I vividly remember showing a slide of the well-known work by Pieter Bruegel the Elder (1525–1569), *The Peasant Wedding*, 1566–1569,[15] in an art history class I was teaching. In the foreground of the painting, two men are carrying a pallet of what appears to be food for a wedding celebration. After viewing this genre painting depicting peasant life in the sixteenth century, a student raised his hand and asked, "What kind of pies are those?" At the time I took the comment to be "off-topic," but I have thought about that comment many times over the ensuing decades and the opportunity I failed to capitalize on. In retrospect, I now realize that the student was seeking more information about the environment he was seeing. He was trying to engage all his senses in the work and enter the painting through smell and taste as well as vision.

Tactile Museums

Many art museums and galleries offer visitors who are blind or visually impaired opportunities to touch original artworks. I have been fortunate to participate in these special experiences at the Philadelphia Museum of Art and the Rodin Museum. With your eyes closed, an educator guides

Figure 7.10 Educators lead sighted visitors, who have agreed to keep their eyes shut, on a tactile exploration of the museum's architecture. This project was initiated by artist Carmen Paplia. http://www.guggenheim.org/video/the-touchy-subject

you through the process of tactily experiencing a sculpture, first taking in its mass and contours and then moving toward the details. It was thrilling and memorable and emphasized to me that tactile experiences can be beneficial for all audiences.

A few years ago, social practice artist Carmen Papalia (b. 1981) facilitated a project with the Guggenheim titled "The Touchy Subject." Papalia "designs experiences that allow those involved to expand their perceptual mobility and claim access to public and institutional spaces."[16] At the Guggenheim, the education department staff participated in a day-long training with Papalia that involved learning how to guide sighted visitors on tactile tours of the museum's art and architecture. Then, on a designated Sunday, visitors were greeted at the entrance and invited to participate in a tactile tour. Those who agreed were paired with an educator. They were then asked to close their eyes and were guided on a short tactile tour of the museum. Both first-time visitors and veterans expressed delight with this one-on-one guided experience.[17] For first-time visitors, it was an unexpected invitation. For those who already knew the museum well, it was an opportunity to experience a familiar place in a novel way.

We used to think of our sensory systems as rather simple, but current research suggests that sensory input plays an even more important role in learning and remembering than previously believed.[18] We are all tactile learners. Opportunities for tactile experiences in art museums should not only be provided for young children and people with visual impairments—but as a valuable addition for all museum-goers.

Chapter 8

Collage, Sculpture, and Manipulatives

"Collage is the twentieth century's greatest creative innovation."—Robert Motherwell[1]

In addition to drawing materials, we have discovered other art materials that have been cleared by our conservation department and deemed acceptable for use in the galleries. This will, of course, vary from museum to museum, so do check with your conservation department whenever considering introducing a new material into your gallery activities.

New materials bring something novel and unexpected to your tours, and any novelty heightens perception and attention. They also allow participants to create a quick response to the work of art you are focusing on.

When working in the galleries, it's best to keep the activities small and relatively quick. Your main focus should remain the works on view in the galleries, not creating a major work of art, so these are relatively quick, informal, and spontaneous responses.

Collage without Scissors or Glue

In introducing collage activities into the galleries, there are two problems that need to be surmounted. How can you make collages without scissors? How can you make collages without glue? The challenge of no scissors can be overcome by precutting collage materials including any papers, fabric, string, and so forth. Avery® Self-Adhesive Lamination Sheets[2] can be a good substitute for glue. Participants arrange their collage materials on a small sheet of cardstock (approximately 4" x 6"), and when they are satisfied with their design, a laminating sheet—cut to size—can be smoothed on top to hold everything in place. Younger students will need some help positioning the laminating sheet, but the process is easily mastered. "Sticky boards," available through art supply vendors, is another commercial product that provides a tacky surface that collage materials will adhere to without the use of glue.[3]

Figure 8.1 In response to the exhibition *Robert Motherwell: Early Collages*, students create collages in the galleries without the use of scissors or glue.

Collage from a Bag

This activity requires some preparation and is most successful as a follow-up to discussions of works of geometric abstraction. Fill a brown paper lunch bag with identical contents of papers cut into geometric shapes in various colors so that each participant receives a bag with the same contents. For instance, one yellow 2" inch right triangle, one green circle, 3" in diameter, one pink rectangle 1" x 2" and so forth—maybe seven or eight shapes in total. In addition to the bag distribute a 4" x 6" piece of card stock—either black or white—that becomes the "canvas." Each participant creates a design. They can augment their shapes by folding and tearing. When they are satisfied with their design, it is secured with a laminating sheet. The designs are then shared.

What I like about this activity is that everyone starts with the same "toolkit"—the same shapes contained within the paper bag—but each participant uses these same materials in his or her own unique way. Seeing how differently these same materials are utilized by each participant adds a new dimension to the discussion as we talk about how, with the same beginning point, we have each created a different design.

Collaborative Collage

This activity provides another option for participants to consider the myriad ways geometric shapes and colors can be arranged on a two-dimensional surface. It can be used in connection with works of geometric abstraction or nonobjective art.

Figure 8.2 Museum educator Jodi Messina-Nozawa leads Guggenheim for All: Reaching Students on the Autism Spectrum. After discussing the painting *Several Circles*, 1926, by Vasily Kandinsky, students take turns placing circles to create a collaborative collage.
PHOTO: FILIP WOLAK

Before or after a discussion, place a large (approximately 20"x 30") piece of paper, oak tag, or foam core in the center of the circle of seated participants. Next to the blank rectangle, place an assortment of differently sized colored papers that have been cut into geometric shapes and lines. This works especially well if the shapes, colors, and lines echo the ones in the work of art the group will be considering. Go around the circle with each participant selecting a paper shape from the pile and deciding where to place it on the white rectangle. As more shapes and lines are added, the composition will become increasingly activated as forms begin to intersect and overlap. Once around the circle, discuss any suggestions for making this a stronger composition. Do things need to be edited, balanced, or adjusted?

Linear Sculpture/Abstraction

A great material to use when looking at linear sculptural works is a gallery-safe, commercially available product known as Wikki Stix.[4] Wikki Stix are precut lengths of yarn that have been

Figure 8.3 Teen visitors create their own mini "flag" or patch of his or her identity by sewing pieces of fabric together in response to *Arms no. 31*, (seen in the background), a tapestry/flag focusing on the history of Taiwan by artist Chia-En Jao. The education department was given permission to use scissors in the galleries for this event.
PHOTO: FILIP WOLAK

coated with wax. The waxy surface enables them to stick to each other and be easily repositioned. I prefer them to either pipe cleaners, which do not adhere to each other, or metal wire, which can be somewhat dangerous in the hands of youngsters. Here are two examples of how they have been used in the galleries.

In 2006, when the David Smith (1906–1965) retrospective was on view at the Guggenheim[5] one of Smith's best-known works, *Hudson River Landscape,*[6] was included in the exhibition. On several occasions, Smith described the genesis of *Hudson River Landscape* as being the product of many drawings that he made while traveling by railroad between Albany and Poughkeepsie.[7] During this period, Smith thought of sculpture not in traditional terms of volume and mass, but as "drawing in space." Although made from steel, it is constructed as linear calligraphy.

We looked carefully at the work and along the Hudson River discussed the elements that seemed to relate to its title. Some participants had taken this trip and pointed out elements that connected to their memories. Some spoke about journeys along other routes.

Following the discussion, participants received an unlined index card and pencil and were asked to close their eyes and remember a landscape that is important to them. It might be a place they see daily, a vacation spot, or a memory from childhood. I then asked them to draw three lines that describe the essence—the character of that place. When the drawings were finished, (maybe

Figure 8.4 Tang Da Wu, b. 1943.
Our Children, 2012.
Galvanized steel, glass, and milk;
three parts: 62 x 89 1/2 x 23 1/2, 26 1/4 x 44 1/2 x 12, and 8 1/2 x 3 1/8 inches (157.5 x 227.3 x 59.7 cm,
66.7 x 113 x 30.5 cm, and 21.6 x 7.9 x 7.9 cm), overall dimensions vary with installation
SOLOMON R. GUGGENHEIM MUSEUM, NEW YORK GUGGENHEIM UBS MAP PURCHASE FUND, 2012
2012.147
© TANG DA WU

about a minute later), each participant got three Wikki Stix and were asked to create a sculptural version of their drawing that describes the essential qualities of that landscape. Although Wikki Stix come in every color imaginable, including fluorescents, I keep the colors low-key, only black or brown, because I don't want the color to be a distraction.

When the sculptures are complete, we discuss them sharing the motivation, process, and outcomes. Participants impart the rich associations they have with these simple structures, and as we hear about the meaning of each line, we learn about the remembered landscape and the human ability to use symbols to create deep meaning. This "lesson" reveals how even a single abstracted line can hold enormous personal significance.

Figure 8.5 Students draw from *Our Children,* 2012 by Tang Da Wu.

In front of another linear sculpture, *Our Children* by Singaporean artist Tang Da Wu,[8] we first discuss the relationship between the two abstracted figures and then take their poses. This work represents an abstracted baby goat kneeling beneath its mother. The work is inspired by a Chinese parable about a young boy's humbling moment of enlightenment at the sight of a kneeling baby goat being fed by its mother. He suddenly understands the sacrifices that parents make for their children. This was particularly apt for family workshops where we asked the adults to "play" the baby goat and the child to take the pose of the adult.

Again, unlined index cards are distributed. This time the drawing prompt is this: "In three lines, portray a relationship that is important to you." When the drawings are finished (maybe about a minute later) each participant gets three Wikki Stix and are asked to create a sculptural version of their drawing that describes the essential qualities of that relationship.

When the sculptures are complete, we discuss them sharing the motivation, process and outcomes. Participants talk about the particular relationship they have depicted and how it is reflected in the sculpture they created. It has been enlightening to see participants describe the rich relationships abstractly portrayed with only three Wikki Stix.

Modeling

Although we frequently feel constrained by the restrictions on the art materials that are allowed in the galleries, during the exhibition, *Peter Fischli David Weiss: How to Work Better*, we were all captivated by their grand collaboration *Suddenly This Overview* (1981–), which was conceived as a "subjective encyclopedia."[9] The entries in this "encyclopedia" take the form of small, unfired clay sculptures on various topics: "popular opposites" (such as work and leisure, in which one worker carries a ladder and the other sits on it); everyday things (snacks); and humorous renditions of historical moments big and small (the first fish decides to go ashore). We yearned for a way to allow our younger visitors to respond to these works through a sculptural material, and then the museum's conservation staff said "yes" to the use of Model Magic®[10] in the galleries. This allowed us to respond to Fischli and Weiss's zany and insightful works in three dimensions.

Manipulatives

Manipulatives are defined as any of various objects or materials that participants can touch and move around. Although frequently used to teach mathematical concepts, touchable, movable materials can be used to reinforce a range of concepts related to visual art, including balance, symmetry, geometry, architecture, and gesture, to name just a few.

In his autobiography, Frank Lloyd Wright (1867–1959), the architect of the Solomon R. Guggenheim Museum and many other important twentieth-century buildings attested to the influence that manipulating Froebel blocks had on the development of his work when he stated, "The maple wood blocks . . . are in my fingers to this day." These wooden blocks were developed in the 1830s by Friedrich Froebel, a German educator and inventor of kindergarten, to help children learn about geometric forms, mathematics, and creative design. Wright was fascinated by them and acknowledged that his architectural designs were influenced by the geometric shapes he experimented with as a child.[11]

Consider adding manipulatives in conjunction with gallery experiences for visitors of all ages. From January to April 2017, the Museum of Modern Art (MoMA) piloted and evaluated a new program, Explore This!, that placed a series of family activity stations in their galleries and invited visitors to participate in various hands-on activities related to works of art on view in their galleries.

Figure 8.6 Architectural experiments with blocks in the galleries.

Figure 8.7 Young visitors participate in a gallery activity in conjunction with the 2006 exhibition, *No Limits, Just Edges: Jackson Pollock Paintings on Paper*. Gestural lines are created using various colors and thicknesses of yarn, ribbon, and string.

Overall highlights from survey responses reported that 100 percent felt their experience with the activity stations had a positive impact on their overall visit to MoMA. Ninety-six percent said the activities helped them connect with and understand art in new ways. In addition, even though the stations were termed "family activity stations," 40 percent said they did not have any children with them on the day they participated. This finding, that many adult visitors welcome the opportunity to participate in activities, is leading MoMA to consider removing the word "family" from their signage to make these opportunities for participation more inclusive.

This study is promising. The ability to participate in gallery activities encourages visitors to spend more time with works of art, consider them more closely, and bring their knowledge and experiences to the task of creating personal meaning. By sitting together in front of works of art, talking about them, and exploring them with all our senses, I sincerely believe that gallery activities can offer a path toward "total immersion" and allow for deeper and more authentic connections with works of art.[12]

Color Palettes and Color Preferences

If there is one style of painting that frequently miffs visitors, it is "Color Field painting,"[13] where a single color or series of unmodulated color panels dominate the work. The lack of figuration, composition, and gestural line sometimes results in visitors asking, "Where's the art?" This activity is designed to get participants thinking about their own color preferences and understanding that the color choices in both Color Field and Minimalist painting are deliberate and carefully selected.

Figure 8.8 Amalia Pica b. 1978,
A ∩ B ∩ C, 2013
Acrylic shapes and occasional performance,
overall dimensions variable,
Solomon R. Guggenheim Museum, New York Guggenheim UBS MAP Purchase Fund, 2014, 2014.45,
© Amalia Pica

The first step in gathering materials for this activity is to visit a home improvement store. Head to the paint department where the paint chips are on display. Take at least one of each. If questioned by an employee, explain that this is for "educational purposes." I have never had a problem and I have a lot of these swatches. Cut them up into individual "color chips." Next you will need two pieces of 9" x 12" white cardstock for each participant. You are now ready.[14]

Following a discussion of the artwork, ask participants, "What is your favorite color?" You will certainly get responses. Five-year-olds and up know their favorite color. But most of us don't think about our favorite series of colors or palette.

Give two pieces of white cardstock to each participant. "On one piece of cardstock, please select four to five color chips that you *love* together. Place them side by side centered on the first piece of cardstock. On the other sheet of cardstock, line up four to five colors that you think are *awful* together." Do not tell the other participants which palette is which. When you have selected both palettes, place them in front of you. We now proceed to look at the palettes in front of each participant. I ask, "How many of you think this is her favorite palette?" Participants who agree raise their hands. I point to the other palette and ask, "How many of you think this is her favorite

Figure 8.9 A young visitor manipulates geometric plastic forms that are miniature versions of the shapes used in Pica's installation.

palette?" Participants who agree raise their hands. The author of the palettes then reveals which are indeed her most- and least-liked color combinations. The interesting thing about this activity is that although the group is frequently correct in their assumptions, they are invariably wrong as well, and assume that the palette that someone hates is the one they totally love.

This activity also forces a reappraisal of colors you normally overlook. It is not easy to select a palette that you really dislike. Try it, you may find that you have a new appreciation for colors you would normally discount. I use this activity with works by Brice Marden (b. 1938),[15] Morris Louis (1912–1962),[16] and Kenneth Noland (1924–2018).[17] It works equally well with other Minimalist or Color Field painters.

Another activity using the same color chips focuses on works by artists who have created abstract paintings inspired by landscapes, where color is an important aspect of the work. Ask participants to close their eyes and imagine a landscape that is important to them. It can be a place they see each day, a memory from childhood, or a favorite vacation spot. In their mind's eye, they should take particular notice of the colors associated with that place. When they open their eyes, ask each participant can choose up to five color chips that suggest the colors of that landscape. Share and discuss these personal palettes as a way to more fully connect with abstract works inspired by nature. A few artists whose work relates to this activity include: Vasily Kandinsky (1866–1944), Josef Albers (1888–1976), Jackson Pollock (1912–1956), Joan Mitchell (1925–1952), Helen Frankenthaler (1928–2011), Cy Twombly (1929–2011), Brice Marden (b. 1938), and Anselm Kiefer (b. 1945), among many others.

Chapter 9

Drama and Movement Activities

"Theater Games are a process applicable to any field, discipline, or subject matter which creates a place where full participation, communication, and transformation can take place."—Viola Spolin[1]

Like many of the ideas in this book, employing the use of movement and drama activities in museum teaching is not new. In various forms, the use of drama and movement to interpret and embody works of art has a long history. The practice may even go back centuries.

Dating back to the 1800s, *tableaux vivant,* literally translated from French, meaning "living pictures," was one of the early popular forms of entertainment used to dramatize, sometimes quite elaborately, works of art. In her article, "Tableaux Vivant: History and Practice,"[2] Shannon Murphy cites the practice of dressing up and acting out scenes from literature, art, or history. Sometimes a poem or music accompanied the scene, and often a large wooden frame outlined the perimeter of the stage, as to reference the frame of a painted canvas. This genre peaked in popularity between 1830 and 1920.[3]

More recently, "Arts Awareness," introduced in the late 1960s by Philip Yenawine, then an educator at the Metropolitan Museum of Art, encouraged students to use words, movements, and sounds to describe works of art and to act out their feelings in response to the art they encountered in the galleries.[4] Concurrently, Susan Sollins, then curator of education at the Smithsonian's National Collection of Fine Arts, used improvisational teaching techniques based on Viola Spolin's theater games as an approach to teaching in the galleries.[5] Writing in 1972, Sollins states,

> The theatre techniques permit a child to experience a work of art visually, physically, emotionally and intellectually. Through this experience, there is a deep involvement with the work of art. In a sense, such an involvement allows children to "climb inside" the painting or sculpture. They know it deeply. Such an experience of art, so very personal with no rights or wrongs, can make art a part of a child's total experience, rather than an extraneous event. The improvisational tour uses [theater] games to focus attention, but the experience generated by game-playing is not a casual one. It is a profound experience of art.[6]

Figure 9.1 Museum educator Amy Rosenblum Martín (bottom) introduces students to the architecture of the museum from a unique vantage point.
PHOTO: FILIP WOLAK

Movement and drama activities can run the gamut from emulating a facial expression or gestures to creating and acting out a full narrative. As you explore the activities on the following pages, keep in mind your own areas of comfort and discomfort and look back over your own teaching experiences.

I am unsure whether to advise you to work on developing the areas of your teaching in which you feel less competent, or suggest that you go with your strengths. While you don't need to be a master in all multimodal approaches, you probably should investigate modalities you would typically shy away from, maybe by seeking out a colleague who is skilled in an area that you would like to develop.

With drama and movement activities, it is particularly important that you understand your audience. For instance, I typically shy away from drama activities with teens. During this developmental phase they are highly self-conscious and aware of their peers. I probably subconsciously remember my own adolescence and how mortified I would have been in being asked to act out a scenario in front of my classmates.

But we recently hosted a drama club from a local high school that made me rethink this bias.[7] I provided a tour of the galleries for the drama club introducing them to various works in our permanent collection. Then each student selected a work of art that appealed to them from those included on the tour. After additional research each student created a short dramatic presentation inspired by the artwork he or she selected, and performed these dramatic pieces in front of the chosen work of art, both engaging visitors and completely dispelling my preconceptions about teens and drama in a museum setting.[8]

The following activities require varied levels of physical participation. As in all the activities outlined in this book, gauge your comfort level, the comfort level of your audience, and consider your goal in including a particular activity on your tour.

Figure 9.2 As part of a family tour, children and adults sing and recreate the movement depicted in the painting *Ring Around the Roses* by Giuseppe Pellizza da Volpedo, completed by Angelo Barabino, *Ring Around the Roses*, ca. 1906/1907–1908. Civica Galleria d'Arte Moderna, Milan.

Tableaux Vivant

As described above, tableaux vivant provides a way for participants to embody the characters pictured in a painting and take on the poses, gestures, and general demeanor of those depicted in the work. Participants can freeze in the scene while others in the group act as coaches helping them to refine their pose. Tableaux vivant can be used for a quick gallery activity or with more research and time can blossom into a full theatrical performance. Adding a prop or costume accessory (like a cane, hat, or shawl—when pictured in the artwork) can add an additional way to embody the subject.

- With a work depicting a single figure: A volunteer emulates the pose of the figure pictured in the work of art. This is actually harder than it sounds, and some gentle coaching from the rest of the group may be appreciated. An extension of this activity would be for other participants to ask the person posing to answer questions while they are "in character." "Who are you?" "How old are you?" "Where are you from?"

Figure 9.3 Edgar Degas (1834–1917),
Dancers in Green and Yellow,
ca. 1903.
Pastel and charcoal on three pieces of tracing paper, mounted to paperboard
38 7/8 x 28 1/8 inches (98.8 x 71.5 cm).

Figure 9.4 Coached by teaching artist Jeff Hopkins, young visitors take the poses of the figures in Henri Rouseau's (1844–1910) painting *The Football Players*, 1908.

- With a work with several figures (see figures 9.3 and 9.4):

  I frequently use this activity in front of a work by Edgar Degas, *Dancers in Green and Yellow*, ca. 1903. The work depicts four dancers, anticipating their cue to come on stage. Each strikes a different pose. One is bent over perhaps adjusting her ballet shoe, another seems confident and relaxed, and another flexes at the knees while still another strains to get a glimpse of the audience.

  We divide into groups of four. I ask that they decide who will take each of the poses to recreate this quartet of dancers. I also ask them to think up a short statement that their character might be thinking, saying, or feeling.

  One at a time, the groups come front and center, recreate the pose of the dancers, and as I point to each participant, one at a time, each recites their line of dialogue. It is interesting to see how each group, working from the same painting, comes up with different interpretations.

- With a work with many figures (see figures 9.5 and 9.6):

  Divide into two groups. Each person takes the pose of a figure in the artwork and decides on what that figure might be thinking or saying. One group "performs" for the other.

Drama and Movement Activities

Figure 9.5 Max Beckmann (1884–1950),
Paris Society, 1931,
Oil on canvas
43 x 69 1/8 inches (109.2 x 175.6 cm)
SOLOMON R. GUGGENHEIM MUSEUM, NEW YORK
70.1927
© 2017 ARTISTS RIGHTS SOCIETY (ARS), NEW YORK/VG BILD-KUNST, BONN

Figure 9.6 During a professional development workshop, teachers mimic the poses in Max Beckmann's painting *Paris Society*, 1931.

At School

If you have an auditorium and are able to project a reproduction of a work on the back of the stage, students can create their own dramatic works based on that work of art. The ultimate embodiment of this approach is probably the 1984 award-winning musical, *Sunday in the Park with George,* that was inspired by the French pointillist painter Georges Seurat's 1884 painting, *A Sunday Afternoon on the Island of La Grande Jatte.*[9]

Tableaux Vivant in Motion

Although the tableaux vivant usually freezes the moment, what might happen if frozen paintings and statues came to life? What would be the next steps of the *Victory of Samothrace,*[10] *Liberty Guiding the People,*[11] or Johannes Vermeer's *Young Woman with a Water Jug*?[12] We may not have these world-renowned artworks in our collections, but no doubt, we have works that would be equally as well-suited to bring to life.

Abstract Sculpture and Painting

Works need not be figurative to be good subjects to animate through creative movement. I have participated in workshops where we brought our bodies to the task of animating a gallery filled with abstract sculptures created by Constantin Brancusi (1876–1957). We each internalized the gesture of a sculpture and then experimented with different possibilities of how each sculpture might move in space.

Kinetic sculptures that actually do move implore us to move with them. We respond to the works of Alexander Calder (1898–1976), George Rickey (1907–2002), and Jean Tinguely (1925–1991), not only intellectually, but viscerally. The expression of that shared mobility can become part of the gallery experience.

Abstract painting likewise presents opportunities for creative movement activities. Try to embody the rhythms, vectors, trajectories, and gestures of shapes and lines embedded in abstract paintings. We have found the Guggenheim's deep collection of works by Vasily Kandinsky a wonderful inspiration for movement activities. The immense variety of lines, shapes, and colors contained in his works provide an almost endless source of potential for gesture and movement from gentle waves to erratic gyrations.

Artist's Process

Imagine that you are creating this painting. How would you move your body to replicate the artist's brushstrokes? Provide a selection of brushes, palette knifes, and so forth that allow participants to choose a tool that demonstrates their "in-air" painting technique. Try this activity with artworks that incorporate a variety of paint applications or try the same activity in front of several paintings with different approaches to paint application.

Before and After

Some works suggest a continuum of action. Although we are seeing a single moment in time, we might be able to imagine what has come before and what will happen next.

Divide participants into small groups and have them work together to create their before and after scenes. These can be done with or without dialogue.

Although we cannot close the curtain or dim the gallery lights for a scene change, I witnessed one educator use this clever technique. When the educator clapped his hands, the "audience" was instructed to close their eyes to provide the "actors" a chance to reposition themselves and move from the "before" scene to the "after" scene. When hands were clapped again, it was a signal to open their eyes for the next scene.

Creating an Abstraction

This activity provides a way to demonstrate and embody the idea of abstraction.

Many twentieth-century artists sought to pare down form to its most basic and elemental structure—its essence. Irene Suris, a former educator at the Guggenheim, would frequently use this activity to help participants understand this process.

She asked the group to recall something they do most mornings to get ready for their day. Some typical responses were, "shower," "make coffee," "get dressed," and so forth. She would then ask for a volunteer to come up and have them act out that task, first in detail, and then getting to the *essence* of that task, paring it down until it was a single motion that embodied that process.

Not all abstract work are efforts to streamline form, but many are, including works by Piet Mondrian (1972-1944), Henri Matisse (1869-1954), Joan Miró (1893-1983), Isamu Noguchi (1904-1988), and Pablo Picasso (188 -1973), among others.

Projecting Emotions

A lightweight 11" x 14" picture frame can be used in conjunction with explorations of portraits to investigate how we read emotions. Used most effectively with younger visitors, after viewing several portraits that depict various emotional states, the educator brainstorms and scribes a short list of emotions with the group—sad, surprised, confused, angry, and so forth. It is very important that the number of emotions is limited to no more than ten, which are written down on a sheet of easel paper and visible to the whole group. Seated in a circle, each participant then holds the frame in front of their face and expresses an emotion from the list. The group attempts to guess the emotion that is being shown. This activity is particularly valued by teachers of students on the autism spectrum who may have difficulty reading emotions.

Storytelling

Story circles use the age-old tradition of storytelling to bring people together. Usually people sit in a circle and present their story ideas. This format creates a space to tell a collaborative story that is inspired by a work of art. For works that have an implied narrative, externalizing, articulating, and extrapolating on that story can provide a collaborative experience.

Select a work with an implied narrative. Explain that we are going to create a collaborative storyline for this work. Every person in the group will speak. You may want to pass around some sort of token that empowers the speaker to contribute to the story—a stone, a detail from the painting (a seashell, tree branch, etc.), or a paintbrush that reminds us that this image was created by a person. Now that our cell phones have built-in audio recorders, it is possible to preserve this collaborative story by passing a cell phone around the circle as each person in the group adds a sentence or two to the narrative. The only rule is that your addition to the story must be grounded in observation of the work of art.

Mindfulness

Although not strictly a movement or drama activity, mindfulness, which is "the practice of maintaining a nonjudgmental state of heightened or complete awareness of one's thoughts, emotions, or experiences on a moment-to-moment basis,"[13] can be used as a productive addition to gallery teaching.

Several Guggenheim educators have investigated how mindfulness can be incorporated into their teaching practice. Instead of asking students to simply "take some time to look at this painting"—the way many educators begin an investigation of a work of art—a mindful approach would be to ask students to "take some time to look at this painting and gather a list of thoughts about what makes it unique and interesting to you."[14]

The use of mindfulness the galleries is particularly appropriate when the works of art have an inherent meditative quality. Guggenheim educators have used these techniques in conjunction with exhibitions by Agnes Martin (1912-2004), V. S. Gaitonde (1924-2001), and On Kawara (1932-2014).[15]

Chapter 10

Sound and Music Activities

"Color is the keyboard, the eyes are the hammers, the soul is the piano with many strings. The artist is the hand that plays, touching one key or another purposely, to cause vibrations in the soul." —Vasily Kandinsky[1]

On January 2, 1911, the artist Vasily Kandinsky (1866-1944) attended a concert of works by the Viennese composer Arnold Schönberg (1874-1951), whose own break with tonal and harmonic conventions paralleled Kandinsky's challenge to figurative art. Kandinsky instantly sensed an affinity between the music and his own move toward abstraction. The two artists began a long-standing friendship and correspondence, drawing inspiration from one another in their search to create new modes of expression.

Kandinsky saw music as the most abstract form of art. He noted that musicians could evoke strong emotions in their audiences through sound and decided that he would strive to create similarly abstract and spiritual paintings.

But Kandinsky is hardly the only artist to explore the connections between music and visual art. Over the centuries, there are many important examples of visual artists who have been inspired by music. Historians have traced this symbiotic relationship back more than five hundred years[2] to works by Piero della Francesca (1415-1492) and Sandro Botticelli (1445-1510), but the relationship between art and music truly blossomed in the twentieth century with the artists Piet Mondrian (1872-1944), Paul Klee (1879-1940), Stuart Davis (1892-1964), Josef Albers (1888-1976), Archibald Motley (1891-1981), Romare Bearden (1911-1988), Jackson Pollock (1912-1956), Robert Rauschenberg (1925-2008), and, of course, Kandinsky, among others that acknowledge the influence of music in their work.

When playing recorded music in the galleries, there are a few things to consider. A musical composition that sounds great in your office may be barely audible when played in the galleries amidst background noise and conversations. Up until recently, I would bring my trusty boombox into the galleries and cue up a track on a CD,[3] since I found it had the loudest volume. Both for ease of carrying, and to avoid social ostracism, I have now converted to playing music from an iPad with the assistance of a clip-on speaker. We have, after some disappointment and experimentation, found speakers that are able to provide the needed amplification, but beware these Bluetooth devices require a strong wifi connection, so be sure to try out your device in the gallery before your tour to ensure all will work smoothly, since "technical difficulties" on your tour can completely disrupt the learning environment you have so diligently worked to create.

As for disturbing other visitors that are not part of your group by playing music in the galleries, I have found that rather than being disturbed, visitors are generally intrigued and delighted to consider these musical connections and sometimes spontaneously join in on the activity.

Some of the activities described below involve bringing recorded music into the galleries. Others focus on creating music or sounds in response to visual works. The introduction of sound and music in response to works of art can be generative, but as in all activities it is important to focus on the following:

- What is your goal in introducing this activity? How might it deepen understanding of this work of art?

- Is this sound/music activity developmentally appropriate for this audience?

- Is this music/sound activity in keeping with the intent of the artist and the artwork?

Synesthesia

At an early age, the artist Vasily Kandinsky exhibited an extraordinary sensitivity toward the stimuli of sounds, words, and colors. His father encouraged his unique and precocious gift for the arts and enrolled him in private drawing classes, as well as piano and cello lessons. However, his decision to become a painter didn't come until he was thirty. In 1896, he attended a concert where he noticed that music could elicit an emotional response without a connection to a recognizable subject. This experience led him to believe that painting should aspire to be as abstract as music.

Kandinsky is believed to have had a neurological condition, chromesthesia, or sound-to-color synesthesia, a type of synesthesia in which heard sounds automatically and involuntarily evoke an experience of color.[4] He developed elaborate theories about how colors could evoke emotions as well as conjure the sounds of musical instruments. However, he also realized that these definitions were not universal. Appendix 2 provides some of Kandinsky's thoughts on color, emotions, and sounds distilled from his 1912 treatise *Concerning the Spiritual in Art*. Accompanying it is a blank table where you can insert your own personal associations with various colors.

The blank table (appendix 3) is compressed to save space. Expand it and provide a copy to each participant. Ask them to complete the form. What emotion(s) does the color yellow suggest to them? What sound(s)? When participants have recorded their responses, take a look at Kandinsky's. When using this activity with adults, try providing Kandinsky's full and quite poetic descriptions of each color and its properties. Responses to color are very personal, and a single color can evoke multiple associations. For instance, red can be loving or fiery or dangerous or celebratory, among many other possibilities.

Choose the Soundtrack

As we see notably demonstrated in movies, the addition of a musical score can influence the way we respond to a visual presentation. This activity can be done with a vast range of artworks, but it requires some preparation. Prior to the tour, choose two pieces of music. They should each complement and support the work of art you will be focusing on, but in different ways. In short, you do not want to choose a "right" and "wrong," but rather two pieces of music that interact with the work of art in different but equally valid ways. For instance, to accompany paintings by Vasily Kandinsky, I frequently play one work by Viennese composer Arnold Schönberg (1874-1951), whose own break with tonal and harmonic conventions paralleled Kandinsky's challenge to figurative art, and another by Alexander Scriabin (1872-1915), a Russian composer and contemporary of Kandinsky's who shared his Russian background and was also influenced by synesthesia.

After a discussion of the artwork, explain to the group that you will be playing two different musical selections that you are proposing to accompany this artwork. Play each for about a minute. Participants may want to jot down a few words so that they can recall their responses to each. You may even need to play each selection twice. By a show of hands, ask the group how many felt that the first selection best complemented the artwork. How about the second selection? Ask supporters of each to explain their reasoning. If using this activity in the classroom, invite students to bring in musical selections they think complement works of art they are studying.

Another variation of this activity, in a gallery that has works of a similar period or style, is to choose a single relevant musical selection by a composer of that same period or style. Have each participant write their name on an index card. Explain that you will be playing some music and would like participants to walk around the gallery and place the index card with their name on the floor in front of the work that they feel has the best synergy with the music. Once all the namecards are placed, walk around the gallery with the group stopping at each cluster of names. Ask participants to explain why they chose that artwork.

Some other possible visual arts and musical pairings include the following:

- Eugène Delacroix (1798-1863) and Frédéric Chopin (1810-1849) shared a friendship and relationship to the romantic trends of the nineteenth century.

- Impressionist paintings are frequently linked with the musical compositions of Claude Debussy (1862-1918), the chief exemplar of musical Impressionism.

- As we look across the history of art, we see that the depiction of music and dance is a major and continuing subject for artists. What type of music might accompany Henri Matisse's painting *The Dance* (1910)? What song might Pablo Picasso's *Three Musicians* (1921) be performing?

- Piet Mondrian (1872-1944) was inspired by the prewar, "hot" jazz and boogie-woogie styles.

- Although known for its revolutionary trends in art, design, and architecture, there was also a Bauhaus band that would come together for dance parties and festivals. "Chairs, gunshots, handbells and giant tuning forks, sirens and pianos prepared by means of nails, wires, and any kind of tone-modifying materials supplemented the instrumental outfit—which consisted by 1928 of some combination of banjos, pianos, percussion, bass (of unclear specification),

Figure 10.1 Joan Miró (1893–1983).
The Tilled Field, 1923–1924,
Oil on canvas
26 x 36 1/2 inches (66 x 92.7 cm)
SOLOMON R. GUGGENHEIM MUSEUM, NEW YORK
72.2020
© 2017 SUCCESSIÓ MIRÓ/ARTISTS RIGHTS SOCIETY (ARS), NEW YORK/ADAGP, PARIS

trombone, clarinet, soprano and alto saxophones."[5] This description seems to provide the museum educator with full permission to interpret Bauhaus works inventively.

- The exhibition, *Stuart Davis: In Full Swing*, that traveled to the Whitney Museum of American Art in New York, the National Gallery in Washington, D.C., and the de Young Museum in San Francisco, highlighted Davis's ability to assimilate the sounds and rhythms of jazz into his work. One can speculate that jazz—especially the music of pianist Earl "Fatha" Hines, his favorite musician, acted as a catalyst for his paintings.[6]

- Jackson Pollock was known to have jazz recordings playing in the background as he created his drip paintings. This music has been made into a compilation featuring tunes from his record collection.[7]

Soundscapes

In addition to works that literally depict the performing arts, landscapes can suggest a variety of sounds. What sorts of noises might accompany Joan Miró's (1893–1983) exuberant and animated surreal worlds like *The Tilled Field*, 1923–1924 (figure 10.1)? What sounds can be imag-

Figure 10.2 Young museum visitors fill the galleries with sound as they explore a work by Carlos Amorales b. 1970, titled *We'll See How Everything Reverberates,* 2012.

ined and created to accompany one of Henri Rousseau's (1844–1910) fanciful inhabited jungles scenes? Have students imagine a sound within a landscape. They can bring them together in a cacophony of various sounds or a "conductor" can be selected, pointing to different participants to contribute their particular sound and orchestrating the impromptu composition.

Soundscapes can also be inspired by abstract works of art. After discussing a work, ask students to find a particular shape, color, or line and create a unique sound that expresses it. Again, the educator is the conductor or invites a volunteer from the group to orchestrate the soundscape.

Percussion Instruments

In addition to creating sounds with our voices and hands, we have a variety of percussion instruments that are occasionally used in the galleries to create sounds and rhythms in response to works on view in our galleries. Occasionally a work will invite visitors to create sounds in the galleries, as we did when this work by Carlos Amorales was on view (figure 10.2).[8]

Chapter 11

Discursive Activities

"Talking in museums is one of the things that makes them matter, and the way in which we talk in museums is one of the things that define for us what they are. Because museums, I think, as much as they are places to go and see things, are also places to go and talk about things, and, through talking, to understand something about the way life takes place in time." —Adam Gopnik[1]

"We asked a number of questions in order to understand viewing habits. One of the interesting conclusions was that people who talk to a companion learn more." —Gary Tinterow[2]

In part I of this book, I explained that gallery activities explore modalities other than talking. So it may seem odd that I am including a chapter on discursive activities—activities devoted to just talking.

Many museum educators use inquiry-based methods as a mainstay of their tours. In response to open-ended questions, for which there can be a multitude of interesting responses, participants focus on various aspects of an artwork verbally offering their perceptions on what they observe (What do you see?), their prior knowledge and experiences (What does this remind you of?), and their personal interpretations (What might this mean?). The discursive activities described here, although they also involve language and speaking, take a different form and veer more closely toward the gallery activity model than the inquiry discussion approach. Discursive activities hold great appeal for all ages—especially adults—and usually require few materials.

Although talking together in the galleries of a museum may seem like a logical expectation and not an occasion of particular note, there are places where conversations of any kind are institutionally and culturally discouraged. While visiting Tokyo, I was quietly speaking with a colleague about a work of art on display when a security guard came over to us to remind us that talking in the galleries was against the rules. There is a large and active museum education community in Tokyo and other parts of Japan that is actively working to change this strongly embedded tradition of appreciating works of art in silence, but it is not easy to change these conventions.

Figure 11.1 Teachers discuss use of color in Vasily Kandinsky's (1866–1944) paintings and their own personal color associations.
PHOTO: FILIP WOLAK

Some of the discursive activities described below involve seeing artworks through a "lens" so that we can perceive a particular aspect of it that may be authentic to our own thinking or even contrary to it. This allows us to "try on" a perspective that is not intuitive to us. So enjoy the freedom of talking to together in the galleries. Below are some examples of discursive activities that primarily focus on just plain talking.

Debate

Debate is a healthy exchange of viewpoints. Unfortunately, according to recent studies, people frequently cling to their beliefs, stubbornly maintaining their viewpoints even in light of new and conflicting information. This phenomenon, termed "confirmation bias," is the tendency to favor information that confirms our existing beliefs and to disavow information that challenges our entrenched positions.[3] The following activity asks us to role-play an assigned point of view even if we disagree with it. It's also a lot of fun.

Make Your Case!

I have seen museum educator David Bowles[4] masterfully facilitate this activity he has dubbed "Make Your Case." The knack is to find a great and provocative quote. At the Metropolitan Museum of Art, a group of adults are seated in front of Georges Seurat's painting *Circus Sideshow* (1887–1888).[5] Of course, the fact that the work hangs at the Met more than a century after it was painted and the name recognition of George Seurat provide an impressive pedigree. David

Figure 11.2 A group discusses Gabriel Orozco's (b. 1962), *Astroturf Constellation,* 2012, composed of 1,188 found objects, including plastic, glass, paper, metal, and other materials collected from a playing field. Dimensions variable.
PHOTO: FILIP WOLAK

dramatically reads to us a quote from an art critic of the time that focuses on how Seurat's work was viewed when it was initially unveiled to the public.

> "Strip his figures of the colored fleas that cover them and underneath there is nothing— no thought, no soul, nothing." —Joris-Karl Huysmans (1848–1907)[6]

We are divided into two groups and assigned positions. Half of the group will support the critic's scathing comments with their own observations. The other half will vehemently refute the validity of the critic's claims. We are provided with a worksheet that asks that we gather visual evidence to support our position. The worksheet encourages us to organize our thoughts by seeing the painting through a different "lens" in order to consider its various aspects: the human figures, the brushstrokes, the composition, and the colors. And then the fun begins. Each time a member of one group defends the painting, the other group presents a counterstatement. We stand and present our arguments with vigor, drama, and conviction. This goes on for quite a while. Taking an assigned position allows us to see another point of view, and dramatizing the delivery of each statement adds an emotional commitment to our proclamations. With a bit of research, many critical statements about well-regarded artists can be found to be used in this activity.

When the Guggenheim Museum first opened, it received both praise and derision. Wright described it as "the unbroken wave," but early critics used other terms, "an inverted potty," "a hangar for flying saucers," "a beehive," and "a corkscrew."[7] These varied metaphors allow us to ask visitors to contribute their own answers to this question: "The Guggenheim is like a . . ."

I have heard "a stack of Frisbees," "a cupcake," and "a washing machine," among many other responses. Today, according to Google, the Guggenheim is the most photographed building in the world.[8] These early quotes from critics—especially the negative ones, provide the viewer with a variety of perspectives and hopefully the freedom and permission to formulate their own personal viewpoints.

Fortunately/Unfortunately

This activity is another form of debate that works well with narrative paintings and can be successful with both adult and youth audiences. The premise is simple. The group is divided in half. One side (the optimists) looks for only positive possibilities from the work. When anyone from this grouping sees something that can be viewed positively, they state it to the whole group. For instance, "Fortunately, it's a sunny day." The other group (the pessimists) meets every positive statement with a negative retort that, for example, begins, "Unfortunately, there are some clouds on the horizon and the weather is about to change." This goes on for as long as the group can "volley" their positive and negative observations back and forth across the group divide. The only rule is that all the statements must be grounded in things that can be observed or deduced from looking at the work of art. I participated when educator Megan Kuensting,[9] facilitated this activity in front of Mark Tansey's painting, *The Innocent Eye Test*, 1981,[10] and was quite amazed by how long we were able to keep this game going.

Look and Describe/Listen and Conjure

Before entering the galleries, have everyone in the group find a partner. One person of this duo will be the "looker/describer," and the other will be the "listener/conjurer." The listener/conjurer is asked to close their eyes until instructed to open them. They are led into the gallery by their partner, who carries two gallery stools; one for each of them. The stools are set up side by side in front of the work of art. The listener/conjurer is seated with their back to the work of art, while the looker/describer faces it. The task of the looker/describer is to verbally describe every aspect of the artwork to their partner in order to provide the most complete description possible. The only thing they are asked not to do is to tell the title of the work or name of the artist. The job of the listener/conjurer is to imagine the image being described to them. When the descriptions are complete, without looking at the artwork, lead a group discussion with only the listeners/conjurers to find out what they learned from the description they just heard, and what they expect this work of art to look like.

Both partners in this activity practice important skills, but the person describing has the more difficult job. They become the eyes for the person who is unable to see, and they are tasked with the responsibility of taking the image they see in front of them and converting that complexity into a comprehensible description. This is an exercise that helps to develop oral literacy.

When the discussion is complete, those who have not seen the image may turn around. This usually prompts another discussion about how the image they conjured is similar to or different from the artwork.

If there is time, repeat the activity in front of another work of art so that the other partner can experience the opposite role.

This activity also works in the classroom. The class is divided in the same way with the lookers/describers facing toward the projection of an artwork, while the listeners/conjurers face away from the screen. In another variation, the listeners/conjurers can draw as they listen to sketch a rough schematic of the work they are hearing described.

Reproduction/Original

Although people come to museums to see original works of art, at times when face to face with a work they have only previously seen in reproduction, they almost can't believe it. Sometimes the experience is sublime, but I have also seen disappointment. I have watched some marvel at the energy and intensity of Vincent van Gogh's *Starry Night* at the Museum of Modern Art, but if you wait just a few minutes, you will also hear the comment, "It's so small!" People travel from far and wide to see visit Leonardo da Vinci's *Mona Lisa* at the Louvre, but in the crowd of admirers will also be some that are underwhelmed. A tour guide reports, "People aren't very happy when they see it. It's too small. They don't believe it's the original."[11]

I can empathize since I have had my own mixed emotions when finally having the opportunity to view the original work of art. Years ago, when people still had printed wall calendars, one month came up with an image of Georgia O'Keefe's *Red Poppy*, 1927. When I learned that the painting was going to be at a New York museum, I imagined myself basking in its glory, enveloped by its deep red tones, and made a plan to visit. I could hardly believe my encounter with the original. At 7"x 9", the painting was smaller than my calendar!

I have also had the opposite experience. The first time I visited Rome's Capitoline Museums, as I climbed the steps to the second floor, I saw a figure I recognized—but in reverse. This was the sculpture of *Dying Gaul*, an ancient Roman marble copy of a lost Hellenistic sculpture. I had studied this work from reproductions in my art history textbooks, but I never considered that *Dying Gaul* actually had a back! From its representation in books, it was always frontal and flat. Seeing it in the round was strangely revelatory. So how can we use this dichotomy between the reproduction and the original in our teaching?

If your museum has postcards of your best-known works, get a stack of them. After discussion of the artwork, distribute the postcards to each participant or have two participants share one. Ask, "What might people only seeing the reproduction miss about this work?" Enjoy the conversation that follows, but don't forget that it is okay for any participant to be more impressed with the reproduction than the original.

Note, this activity can also be used as a previsit orientation where the reproduction is shared prior to the visit and participants compare the experience of the postcard with viewing the original work in the museum. Some teachers have expressed concern to me that if students see a reproduction of the work prior to their visit, they will be less interested in viewing the work of art in the museum. I have found exactly the opposite to be true. The more we are familiar with the works of art we will encounter, the more we will be interested in seeing the original. Advertising capitalizes on this psychology by inundating us with coming attractions, previews, and trailers for new film and television releases. Knowing something in advance about what will be seen on a museum visit can greatly support and stimulate interest.

Looking through "Lenses"

Some works of art have so much visual information in them that it is difficult to take it all in. A work that fits this description is Thomas Hart Benton's *America Today*,[12] 1930–1931. Offering a panorama

Figure 11.3 Teachers at the Metropolitan Museum of Art discuss Thomas Hart Benton's (1889–1975) mural, *America Today*, 1930–1931. Photo by Filip Wolak/The Metropolitan Museum of Art
https://www.metmuseum.org/art/collection/search/499559
PHOTO: FILIP WOLAK

of life in the United States throughout the 1920s, *America Today* is a room-sized mural comprised of ten panels that are permanently installed in a gallery at the Metropolitan Museum of Art.

To create it, Benton traveled across the country documenting varied aspects of life, from factories to dance halls, cotton field workers to subway riders. To help facilitate careful looking, museum educator Claire Moore[13] divided our tour group into four subgroups. We were given paper, a pencil, and the task of looking at the work through a particular lens, either "labor," "technology," "entertainment and culture," or "social issues," with the instruction to jot down or sketch images from the mural related to the lens you were assigned. After about five minutes, we got back in our groups, discussed, and aggregated our findings and then shared them with the whole group. The use of the lens allowed for closer looking and appreciation of Benton's achievement. The process of talking together allowed us to consider aspects of the work that would have otherwise gone unnoticed. This strategy can be applied to other complex works so that viewers can appreciate and digest them in smaller "bites."

Match the Color

I observed museum educators Hollie Ecker and Sarah Mostow[14] use this strategy of "matching the color" as a warm-up activity as they introduced a group of students to the galleries. Each student selected a favorite color from a large assortment of color chips acquired from the paint department of a local hardware store. The students were then asked to circulate through the gallery of paintings looking for a color that matched their color chip in one of the artworks. Most students were able to locate a matching color and then described their process and, without pointing at the painting (we prefer to use words), described the location of "their" color.

Look and Recall

Look and recall is another warm-up activity that works best with figurative works that have a lot going on in them. Invite the group to look at the work for a few minutes. Then ask them to turn their back to the painting. Go around the group in turn, asking each participant to recall something from the painting. How many nonrepetitive things can they recall? I have tried this activity in two ways. Sometimes I have asked the group to look at the painting without letting them know they will be asked to recall details, or you can announce, "You have two minutes to look at this painting and remember as much as possible of what is in front of you. Then we will turn away from the work and see how much we can recall." The two approaches yield different results, but both can be successful.

Whichever approach you use, keep a written log of the responses. Ask participants to discuss anything they noticed by doing this activity of which they had not previously been aware.

Using Adjectives

Provide each participant with the same list of approximately thirty disparate adjectives. An adjective is a word that modifies a noun (or pronoun) to make it more specific. Some examples: *colorful, natural, delicate, free, chaotic, polite*.[15] Then set the group free in a gallery asking each person to choose his or her favorite artwork—but not telling which one they selected. Circle three adjectives on the list that best describe this artwork. (A bit of subterfuge is needed here so others don't see you standing in front of the work.) When the group reassembles, a participant shares the adjectives they have selected. See if others in your group can guess the chosen work using only these three adjectives as clues. Once the artwork is located, a discussion can ensue about why these words were selected and how these adjectives were helpful in identifying the work. This is a nice family activity where an adult and child can exchange their circled adjectives and hunt for the work the other has selected.

A variation of this activity is done in front of a single work. Participants are given the same list of adjectives and asked to circle the three words that they feel are the best descriptors. The key here is to select a work of art that suggests multiple possibilities. For instance, some people may find works by Joan Miró *eerie* while others will see them as *playful*. Visitors may think Vasily Kandinsky's late abstractions are *chaotic* while others will call them *lyrical*. These adjectives can provide the basis for a discussion about these differences in individual perceptions.

A Focus on Place

There are artists who return again and again to painting a particular place. Camille Pissarro (1830–1903) painted the French town of Pontoise in every season; Paul Cézanne (1882–1906) created more than sixty paintings of Mont Sainte-Victoire,[16] and Georgia O'Keeffe (1887–1986) focused her work on New Mexico's landscape for decades. These are just a few of the artists who have pursued an ongoing exploration in a singular place.

With our ability to instantly call up images on the internet, the educator can provide photographs of these inspirational locales and use them to prompt discussions of how the artist has conveyed their unique vision of this place. In my own teaching, I frequently use a set of photographs that a colleague took on a trip to Paris that documents Édouard Vuillard's *Place Vintimille* (1908–1910). Vuillard found endless fascination in this park that he saw from his Paris apartment window, and being able to view this park over the span of a century invariably prompts lively conversations about what has changed and what has stayed essentially the same.

Civil Discourse

In recent years there have been increasing discussions about the role that museums can play as sites for public forums and promoting social justice. From racial injustice to climate change, from gun control to immigration, we grapple with the complex and divisive issues of our time. Although I differ with those who believe that museums are perceived as neutral or safe spaces for all, through discourse, museums can be places for constructive discussions and collaborative meaning-making through dialogue-based programs.[17] In discussing works of art that contain political or social content, externalizing the focus on the artwork, rather than on individually held beliefs, can allow for the sharing of varying perspectives and a more open exchanges of ideas.

A word of caution is in order. In interviewing visitors, some hold the view that museums should be apolitical and remain places of respite, beyond the fray of the world outside. This is the very reason they have decided to visit an art museum. When the conversation moves toward more political subjects, they may feel that things are straying "off topic." They came to the museum, in part, to get away from the issues of the day, not to engage in conversations about them and with people they don't know well.

If you know that the works you are selecting have political and social content, it might be wise to mention that at the beginning of the gallery experience. "I have selected works by artists who are examining the issues of our time, just like we all are. I will be interested in hearing what you think." Hopefully this early acknowledgment will help pave the way for everyone on your tour to feel a bit more informed about what to expect.

The Whip Around

The whip-around activity involves careful looking combines both writing and talking. For a full description see chapter 5, "Writing Activities" on page 29.

Chapter 12

Digital Media Activities[1]

"Technology is just a tool. In terms of getting the kids working together and motivating them, the teacher is most important." —Bill Gates, founder of Microsoft[2]

"If your museum lost power, how would that affect the learning experience in the galleries and across programming?" —Mike Murawski, founding editor of ArtMuseum Teaching.com[3]

Museums are being redefined for a digital age. According to the Pew Research Center's Internet & American Life Project,[4] digital media has influenced just about every aspect of museums, from how art is presented to how it is experienced. "The internet, social media, and mobile connectivity now permeate their operations and have changed the way they stage performances, mount and showcase their exhibits, engage their audiences, sell tickets, and raise funds."[5]

Many museums are investing in technology as the interpretive tool of choice with the belief that it holds the most appeal for younger audiences. The ability to call up a video of the artist speaking about a work of art, or the curator describing their exhibition decisions can add a powerful dimension to contextualizing the works on view.

More and more museums not only allow visitors to use their mobile phones while browsing the artworks on view, they encourage it. Our visitors cruise exhibitions with their smartphone cameras poised. They listen and interact with multimedia guides and scan QR codes. Indeed, digital media is pervasive in nearly every aspect of the contemporary art museum, except for one. Most educator-led tours have remained relatively free from these technological innovations.

Depending on your own relationship with digital media, you may see this as a positive factor or a sign that this area of audience interaction has been left behind. In his 2013 post, museum educator Mike Murawski asks, "Are We Becoming Too Reliant on Technology?"[6] The question of whether the guided gallery tour should be one that skillfully integrates digital technology or remain a tech-free zone is one that each gallery teacher needs to consider for themselves. If your response is "maybe," this chapter provides some strategies for integrating digital media into educator-facilitated tours.

For anyone who has watched museum visitors using digital devices, you will find that they are participating in a singular and individual learning experience rather than a social one. Participants have their headphones on listening, looking, and no doubt learning, but they are in their own world. I have even seen a couple in our café, sitting across from each other having lunch, with their headphones on.

In an informal evaluation of the Guggenheim Museum's multimedia guide, this observation was confirmed. We provided a group of preteens with a device loaded with a multimedia guide designed for youth and then followed them through the museum. Although they enjoyed pushing the buttons, hearing the descriptions, and moving on to the next work of art, we noticed how little they actually looked at works of art and interacted with each other. The guide became an individual scavenger hunt to find the next artwork, listen to the narration, and then move on. How can we encourage more "look-up" experiences—up at the art instead of down at a smartphone or tablet?

Some museum professionals are concerned that an overemphasis on technology is displacing human interaction to the detriment of visitor experience.[7] One of the major goals for interactive tours is to support learning and engagement, but another important reason people decide to take an educator-led tour is the possibility of social interaction. How can we strategically incorporate digital media into tours without losing the interpersonal connections? The activities offered below are an attempt to use the power and allure of digital media but still provide the social interactivity and collaborative learning opportunities that any good gallery tour should provide.

Digital applications and media can be used across many of the modalities that are considered in this book, including writing, drawing, collage, and sound, and so forth, but given the barrier of entry with digital activities, the question the educator needs to ask themselves is this: "When does it make sense to incorporate digital media into the gallery tour?" Focusing on what's unique about digital media (that it's easy to copy, store, share, modify) compared to analog technologies, can help the educator to think critically about when digital makes sense, and when it doesn't.

Videos

I distinctly remember the first time I saw an iPad used as a tool for gallery teaching. It was July 2010 at the Whitney Museum of American Art. Museum educator Ai Wee Seow[8] was facilitating a conversation about Andy Warhol's (1928–1987) *Dance Diagram, 5 (Fox Trot: "The Right Turn—Man")* 1962.[9] The work, designed to be installed on the gallery floor, appropriates a diagram showing how to do a basic dance step. Aiwee then pulled out an iPad, pressed a button, and showed a video of a couple gliding across a dance floor doing the fox trot. The message was clear. A new and powerful teaching tool was now available to museum educators to integrate into guided gallery experiences.

Since then I frequently pack an iPad into my tote bag of teaching materials, enabling me to include short interviews with artists, share documentation of their process, and view time-lapse installation clips. Although these inclusions are not technically gallery activities, if strategically used, they can prompt additional dialogue, closer looking, and new insights.

With the enormous resources of the internet at your disposal, it is important to be discerning about your selections. Be sure to test out any videos before your tour to ensure that you have

Figure 12.1 Participants in the museum's *Mind's Eye* program for visitors with vision loss and blindness view contextual photographs on an iPad. Notice the use of assistive listening devices to amplify sound.

both the volume and connectivity to avoid unpleasant technical glitches. Keep any video segment short, and always use them to prompt additional conversations.

Digital Postcards

Long ago, in a predigital age, when you went on vacation, you would mail postcards to friends and relatives telling them about the new places you were visiting and experiences you were having. On the flip side of your handwritten message would be a photograph or drawing of the vacation spot.

With today's instantaneous communication, this tradition has faded, replaced by digital photos, postings, and messages (although I still have a few young friends who enjoy receiving a mailed postcard).

Chapter 5, which focuses on writing activities, includes a description of how writing a postcard can help tour participants reflect on their museum experience. Request that each participant mentally choose an intended recipient and write about what they have just seen and learned. This helps to both distill and clarify what each participant values. Then ask volunteers to share their writing. Whom did they choose to write to and why?

This activity can also be implemented digitally. Encourage participants to take photos on their smartphones at designated intervals during the tour. At the end of the tour, each participant takes a few minutes to create a digital postcard, through email, by texting, or with one of the many free applications for creating digital postcards. Facilitate a discussion about which image was selected, what message will be sent and to whom, and of course, what determined these decisions.

Padlet

Padlet is a free tool that can be used to create an online bulletin board that you can use to display information on any topic. It is available at https://padlet.com/. You can add images, links, video, and more to your digital bulletin board, or "wall," as Padlet calls it. They can be private, open to the public, or moderated by you—meaning that you approve all contributions before they are displayed. The analog equivalent might be a giant poster pad that has room to accommodate responses from a large (actually infinite) number of respondents, and you don't need to be the scribe. By providing the URL for your particular Padlet, users can contribute to the collective bulletin board.

Some advantages to using Padlet include the following:

- The barrier of entry is fairly low; you do not need accounts to create or contribute to a Padlet wall, and it's accessible on desktop computers, tablets, and smartphones.

- Contributors can easily add text, pictures, videos, links, and documents to collaborate and respond to one another in real time. All they have to do is double-click or tap anywhere on the wall to add a "Post-It" note.

- Padlet walls are infinite in size, yet each sticky note is limited to 150 characters, so contributors can share many ideas or resources in short succession.

Padlet can pose an open-ended question in order to elicit multiple responses—a natural fit for collective discussions in front of works of art. We have used Padlet during an educator workshop focusing on works by Carrie Mae Weems (b. 1953) and again to solicit responses from teens on works they viewed during an informal "Teen Night" at the museum. An easy way to experiment with Padlet is to give it a try with a simple open-ended question that lends itself to multiple responses. As users become more accustomed to how Padlet functions, they will also get more comfortable posting their unique responses.[10]

Smartphones/Photos

In 1973, the cultural analyst and writer Susan Sontag wrote, "Needing to have reality confirmed and experience enhanced by photographs is an aesthetic consumerism to which everyone is now addicted. Industrial societies turn their citizens into image-junkies; it is the most irresistible form of mental pollution."[11] If we were image junkies in 1975, what are we now?

Figure 12.2 Students in the museum's afterschool program use iPads to photograph an exhibition by artist Wang Jianwei, b. 1958.

According to a 2016 *New York Times* article, you can count on most visitors to your museum who are over the age of ten having a smartphone with them, and the age of smartphone users/owners is only expected to get younger.[12] We may agree or disagree with this trend, but there is no denying that this tool has influenced how we visit museums. And so it is up to the museum educator to decide whether the museum experience they construct will be a device-free or device-friendly one.

Although there is still scant research on impact on the museum experience as filtered through smartphones, one study[13] suggests that if participants are asked to zero in on a detail that interests them, rather than the entire work of art, their memory of that work is enhanced. The researchers think that the improvement is due to a more personal interaction with the object.

Taking photos of entire artworks documents that you have been in close proximity to it, but not necessarily that you looked at it carefully, but in selecting details to photograph the visitor needs to look, think, and select something of interest. This process of selection may allow for greater memory retention, so keep this difference in mind as you design your activities.[14]

These findings suggest that it may be more fruitful to ask participants to share a detail of a work of art they have captured, rather than photographing the entire work. When sharing these details, ask participants what led them to zoom in on that detail. What was compelling about that particular element?

Smartphone cameras can be used in a numerous ways. In front of a visually complicated work of art, participants can be asked to select and photograph a detail that particularly interests them. Likewise for large sculptural works, participants can use their smartphone cameras to capture a particular point of view that they find compelling.

Armed with their smartphone, participants can be sent out on "missions" and return to the group with their "findings" captured in photos to be shared and discussed. Provide the group with a prompt so that they are all seeking to answer the same question. Some possible prompts: "Take the next five minutes to find a work of art in this gallery that puzzles you; that you would like to find out more about; that you have greatest connection with; and so forth. Once you have settled on the work, take a photo of it and the object label that accompanies it (and maybe some details as well). Bring it back to the group. As much as participants enjoy the group dynamic of being part of a tour, this activity also allows them to do some individual exploring with a common purpose, and then share their discoveries with the group.

Smartphones/Audio Recording

Interviews are powerful learning opportunities. Young people interviewing adults can provide opportunities to ask questions of "grown-ups" that they would not otherwise have. Having adults interview children provides uninterrupted listening time and acknowledges that the viewpoints of young people are worth documenting, listening to, and considering.

Drawing Applications

Gallery experiences that use drawing apps can be engaging across age groups, but there a few steps to planning that will help things to go smoothly.

- Try out some free drawing applications.[15]

- The group should know in advance that you will be doing digital drawing during the tour.

- As in all interactive tours, provide gallery stools for participants.

- Reserve time at the beginning of the tour for everyone to download the application onto their phone or provide participants with iPads that have the app preloaded. If possible, provide download information in advance of the tour in your marketing materials or tour description.

- Take a few minutes before the tour begins for the participants to experiment with using the app. How do you get a clean page, choose the color and width of your line, or save your work? Getting the group acquainted with the interface before you begin your tour will allow the group to focus on the works of art and their drawings rather than on how to use the tool. All of this takes time and effort in comparison with the very direct act of drawing on paper with a pencil, but when we used a digital drawing tool on a regular basis with elementary school students, we found that over time, students became more confident in their drawing because the stakes were lower. If you make a mistake, you can easily correct or undo it. This confidence appeared to transfer over to nondigital mediums as well.[16]

- Realize that you are doubling your responsibilities. You are teaching both responsiveness to works of art and getting comfortable with a new digital tool.

- When deciding on your tour stops, it is best to select more abstract works. We are not going for realism here, but rather getting in touch with line quality, mark-making, gesture, and contour.

- Remind everyone that it takes some time to master anything new. With a bit of time and patience, they will become more comfortable and satisfied with their creations.

Audio Recording and Editing

Recording and editing ambient noise is another way of interpreting one's experience in the museum and can be done with relative ease using a smartphone or tablet. As with digital drawing activities, it's important to try out different sound editing apps before deciding to use them on a tour. GarageBand is a free, popular app available on iOS that we have used at the Guggenheim with both adult and youth groups. As an educator, you should know how to introduce visitors to the basics and help them troubleshoot any challenges that may arise, but you don't have to know everything about an app (and you will likely learn from your tour attendees!). Given that people have different levels of experience with audio editing, it's helpful to have visitors work in pairs or groups to record and edit sounds so they can support and learn from one another throughout the process. It's also important to provide a creative prompt and a time limit for the length of the final recording; both will encourage attendees to be intentional throughout the editing and recording process, and the time limit will ensure that everyone will have enough time to share and reflect on their work with the broader group. In our tours at the Guggenheim, we limited audio recordings to thirty and sixty seconds.

Digital Galleries

A hashtag is word or phrase preceded by the symbol pound symbol (#) that classifies or categorizes the accompanying content so that it can be shared on a social media platform. It allows participants to digitally post their work under an overarching theme. This option, to impart your creation to a much larger audience, adds another dimension to the concept of "sharing." In deciding on any thematic "umbrella," it is important for it to be both inclusive enough to allow for diversity, but also unique and exclusive enough to provide for a degree of cohesion. For instance, for a day of drawing the architecture of the three Guggenheim museums in New York, Venice, and Bilbao, we worked with our marketing team to add the hashtag #DrawingtheGuggenheim so that anyone interested in posting a drawing could add it under this hashtag.

In 2015, the Rijksmuseum in Amsterdam launched #hierteekenen (or "Start Drawing"),[17] a similar initiative to encourage visitors to slow down and sketch the works they see in the galleries instead of photographing them. By adding a hashtag, the museum is actually promoting more analog interpretation strategies by using a digital tool. The posting option will be enticing to some and superfluous to others, but it greatly broadens and aggregates the possible reach of the work created within your tour.

Chapter 13

One Work/One Activity

"The whole audience of art is an audience of individuals. Each of them comes to the painting or sculpture because there he can be told that he, the individual, transcends all classes and flouts all predictions. In the work of art, he finds his uniqueness confirmed."
—Ben Shahn (1898-1969)[1]

In deciding to write this book, my goal was to make it as usable as possible by concentrating on activities that can be applied to many works of art and multiple audiences, but there is another category of activities that bears mentioning. Sometimes you will be studying a new exhibition and an artwork suggests an activity that is unique to that work. If that work is in a changing exhibition, you may only be able to use it for a few months, but those unique works and activities can create memorable experiences for both you and your audiences, and so I am closing this book by recounting a few of those favorite, but now shelved, activities that had a brief moment of application, but may forever more be relegated to the "archive of dormant gallery activities." They are unique because the work of art they were developed to support is unique. They are successful because they are custom-tailored to a particular work of art. Because these activities have limited application, I have selected only a few out of scores of these activities as a way of sharing how they uniquely supported a specific work of art. This chapter is also meant to encourage other educators to respond to new works of art by developing your own unique activities for the works on view in your institutions.

A Writing Activity for *Index*, a work by Alejandro Cesarco

During the summer of 2014, the exhibition *Under the Same Sun: Art from Latin America Today* was on view in the Guggenheim's galleries. The show reconsidered the state of contemporary art in Latin America. This group show included *Index*, a work by Alejandro Cesarco (1975-).[2] If you were to encounter this work in the galleries, most people would walk right by it. It consists of twelve framed pieces of paper with typed words. In galleries filled with large, bold, and colorful works, you could miss Cesarco's contribution entirely. On closer examination, however, these pieces of paper reveal an entire life. On these pages, Cesarco has written the index of his imaginary autobiography. The book remains unwritten, but if we take the time to examine its index, we get a full self-portrait of the author's aspirations, influences, and interests.[3] For instance, under the letter "J," Cesarco has entries for Jealousy; Joy; Judd, Donald; and Justice; among others. Under "M," we notice Madame Bovary; Magritte, René; Masculinity; Mediation; Melancholia; and Museum.

According to the artist, this was an "Index of a book I haven't yet written and most probably never will. A container that becomes its own content. The index is half way biographical and half way theory text; it is extremely personal, at times even hermetic, yet full of clichés."[4]

This idea of constructing an index for your own autobiography seemed like an apt follow-up to deeply considering this work. The tour group was invited to get close enough to read the work. After a few minutes of looking and reading, I asked them what they had learned. They recounted various entries and also began to extrapolate about the personality and interests of the artist/author.

And then I gave them a sheet of paper with letters of the alphabet, A to Z with space in between to begin to create their own *Index*. We worked on this for a while and then discussed how we went about thinking about our lives. Some participants began chronologically, beginning at their earliest memories; others worked from their current priorities. We talked about the memories, issues, and influences that came to mind as they worked on their personal index. This simple activity paralleled and supported the artist's work and helped us all to connect more deeply with Cesarco's autobiography and our own.

Using a Manipulative to Embody Saburo Murakami's Work *Passage* (1956)

In 2013, the Guggenheim mounted *Gutai: Splendid Playground*,[5] the first U.S. retrospective exhibition devoted to Gutai, an influential artistic movement that emerged in Japan following World War II. One of the central ideas of Gutai was to break through traditional limits and explore new ways to create art. In the exhibition was a mural-size photograph documenting a seminal performance work *Passage*,[6] (1956) by Murakami Saburō (1925–1996). The photo shows Murakami in the process of propelling himself through taut paper screens resembling large canvases, but stretched with paper rather than canvas. His work is a metaphor for breaking boundaries of conventional artistic limits. He crashed through this series of paper screens so violently that he landed with a concussion, but somehow the still photograph failed to convey the true difficulty and intensity of this act.

After a discussion of the work, museum educator Queena Ko[7] distributed a brown paper lunch bag to each participant and asked them to break through the bottom of the bag. We were all surprised by how difficult it was. Some needed to apply forceful, repeated punches to rupture the bag. The activity allowed us to have a more visceral sense of what the artist must have experienced and changed our understanding of the work from a purely intellectual one, to an experiential (but still safe) one. It is also in keeping with the experimental nature of the artwork.

In his writing, Murakami urges us to "Follow the rules. . . . Rules between nations. Traffic rules. Rules about money. . . . But when you draw a picture or make a poem, you are in your own world, so no matter how fast you drive, you don't have to worry about killing anyone or hurting other people. . . . In the world of art and poetry, there are no rules. . . . When you draw pictures and write poems, please exceed the speed limit as much as you like."[8]

The Use of a Touch Object with Antonio de Pereda's painting, *Vanitas*[9]

Sometimes the perfect touch object presents itself. I was given a human skull (sans its mandible) by a retired dentist, which I was able to put to good use during tours of *Spanish Painting from El Greco to Picasso: Time, Truth, and History*.[10] Included in the show was a small painting by Antonio de Pereda (1611–1678) titled *Vanitas*. Vanitas are a type of still-life paintings that incorporate objects symbolizing the fleeting nature of life, such as decaying fruit, withering flowers, skulls, hourglasses, or musical instruments.[11] Pereda was one of the most outstanding *vanitas* painters of his time. In this work, we see a pocket watch and three skull-like forms, but I noticed that sometimes tour-goers were confounded by unusual positioning of the skulls. "Is it some other kind of animal?" "I only see one eye." I even heard, "It might be a rotting melon." The problem in understanding the perspective is that Pereda painted one of the skulls from below, as though we are looking up through the hole in the base of the skull through which the spinal cord passes (foramen magnum).

And then, from the bag of materials I carry with me on each tour, I pull out a human skull and pass it around the group. Holding the object and looking at its base instantly clarifies what is going on in the painting. Pereda has perfectly rendered the skull from below, and it is clear that the group has a better understanding of the image and another unique experience: the opportunity to examine a human skull.

Figure 13.1 Christopher Wool, *Black Book Drawings*, 1989, installation view.
FROM CHRISTOPHER WOOL, OCTOBER 25, 2013-JANUARY 22, 2014, SOLOMON R. GUGGENHEIM MUSEUM
PHOTO: DAVID HEALD

Figure 13.2 Mount Sinai School of Medicine students and faculty use stencils to add another word to Wool's series.
PHOTO: CHAD HEIRD

A Writing and Drawing Activity Inspired by Christopher Wool's *Black Book Drawings*

A 2003 Christopher Wool (b. 1955) retrospective included his *Black Book Drawings*, a suite of twenty-two works on paper.[12] Each work contained a nine-letter word/image in bold capital letters, divided into three lines containing three letters each. The words loosely focus on negative personality traits. Examples include: PAR-ANO-IAC; PSY-CHO-TIC; EXT-REM-IST; HYP-OCR-ITE; and my favorite, ASS-ASS-IN. The language in Wool's paintings is often treated as much as abstract shapes as words with a communicative function. They are not subject to conventional spacing or punctuation rules. Reading them for meaning can often be like putting together a puzzle.[13] Although this is not a work I would use with young children, with adults it provided for great discussions and an opportunity to think about what nine-letter word you would want to add to this suite of drawings.

For this activity, I created a template that was exactly proportional to Wool's format and provided block letter stencils that would yield a similar result on the page. The word choices that the participants drew into their templates were wonderfully in keeping with Wool's acerbic aesthetic, including APA-THE-TIC; CON-CEI-TED; MAL-ICI-OUS; and TAS-TEL-ESS. This activity helped us look, think, and participate more fully in this work.

A Collage Activity for Gabriel Orozco *Astroturf Constellation*

To create *Astroturf Constellation*,[14] artist Gabriel Orozco (b. 1962) collected, sorted, categorized, and displayed a table installation with 1,188 tiny found objects, including plastic, glass, paper, metal, and other materials. The objects include coins, bottle caps, cigarette butts, wads of chewing gum, candy wrappers, and a feather, among many other bits of detritus. These are pieces of garbage that Orozco collected from the Astroturf field where he likes to throw boomerangs and play soccer on Manhattan's Pier 40. As he does with many of his works, Orozco applies his personal aesthetic and sorting sensibilities to what others would simply see as garbage.

It took me a while to collect the materials for this activity. For a few weeks I walked around head down, foraging for tiny pieces of trash, filling my pockets and then carefully washing my haul and

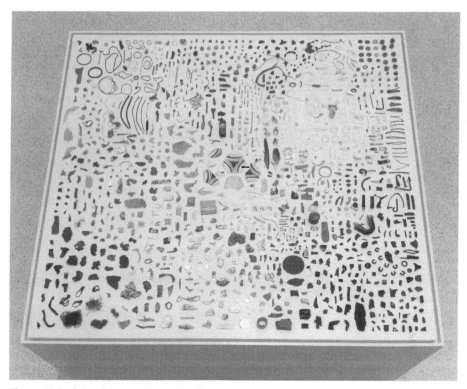

Figure 13.3 Gabriel Orozco, b. 1962, Jalapa, Mexico,
Astroturf Constellation, 2012,
1,188 found objects, including plastic, glass, paper, metal, and other materials
dimensions variable.

SOLOMON R. GUGGENHEIM MUSEUM, NEW YORK COMMISSIONED BY DEUTSCHE BANK AG IN CONSULTATION
WITH THE SOLOMON R. GUGGENHEIM FOUNDATION FOR THE DEUTSCHE GUGGENHEIM, BERLIN
2012.204.1-29
© GABRIEL OROZCO

Figure 13.4 Participants experiment with various ways that small
found objects can be arranged.
PHOTO: FILIP WOLAK

eventually collecting enough debris to use in the galleries. The only other materials needed were 20" x 20" pieces of white illustration board to set down on the gallery floor to serve as temporary "tables."

Tour participants were fascinated by this work. Once you begin to recognize what it is made from, you want to identify the origins of every fragment. The work transforms from something conceptual to extremely accessible and viewer-friendly.

I decided that this would be an interesting activity to do in groups since there are a number of possible ways to arrange these individual pieces of "schmootz," and negotiating the "sorting logic" would be an interesting conversation. What type of taxonomic arrangement would each group agree on: color, material, size, or some other criteria? Each group of four got a piece of illustration board and a generous handful of stuff. The activity made apparent the vast number of ways that unlike things can be organized.

Conclusion

I doubt I will ever have the opportunity to use any of these activities again since they are completely unique to the work they were designed to support, but the process of creating them and trying them out with willing visitors has been great fun. I invite and encourage all of you to invent new activities for the works that appear, even fleetingly, in your galleries.

Appendix 1

Lesson Plan Template[1]

Educator: _____

Tour Theme: _____

Describe how this theme is relevant to the group with which you are working.

Advance organizer:[2]

Object (artwork) selections:

Work 1:

Artist:

Title, date:

Materials:

Open-ended questions related to this artwork in the sequence they would be presented.

1.

2.

3.

Important information about this artwork that is related to the theme.

1.

2.

3.

Activity for this artwork (multimodal approach):

This template would be completed for each of the three to five works in your tour.

Group reflection:[3]

Appendix 2

Synesthesia Table Condensed from the Writings by Vasily Kandinsky.[1]

Color	Emotion	Sound
Yellow	"Warm," "cheeky and exciting," "disturbing for people," "typical earthly color"	Loud, sharp trumpets, high fanfares
Blue	Deep, inner, supernatural, peaceful, "typical heavenly color"	Light blue: flute Darker blue: cello Darkest blue: organ
Green	Stillness, peace, but with hidden strength, passive	Quiet, drawn-out, middle position violin
White	"It is not a dead silence, but one pregnant with possibilities."	"Harmony of silence," "pause that breaks temporarily the melody"
Black	Eternal silence, without future and hope." Extinguished, immovable	"Final pause, after which any continuation of the melody seems the dawn of another world."
Gray	"Immovability, which is hopeless"	Soundless
Red	Alive, restless, confident, strength, energy, joy	"Sound of a trumpet, strong, harsh" Fanfare, tuba Deep notes on the cello High, clear violin
Brown	Mixture of red and black; dull, hard, inhibited	"Barely audible, but a powerful inner harmony"
Orange	Mixture of red and yellow; radiant, healthy, serious	Middle-range church bell, alto voice, "an alto violin, singing tone, largo"
Violet	Mixture of red and blue; "morbid, extinguished [. . .] sad"	English horn, bassoon

Appendix 3

Synesthesia Table: Blank

	Color	Emotion	Sound
Yellow			
Blue			
Green			
White			
Black			
Gray			
Red			
Brown			
Orange			
Violet			

Notes

Preface

1. Gallery activities are also referred to as nondiscursive activities, multimodal activities, responsive activities, or participatory techniques.
2. Olga Hubard, 2015. "Art Museum Education: Facilitating Gallery Experiences," Chapter 9, Complete Engagement: Embodied Response and Multimodal Facilitation, Palgrave Macmillan, NY. 125. This important essay is also available online at: https://artvolunteers.wikispaces.com/file/view/Complete+Engagement-+Embodied+Response+in+Art+Museum+Education.pdf
3. Susan Sollins, "Games Children Play: In Museums," *Art Journal* 31, no. 3 (Spring 1972), 271–75.
4. Sollins, "Games Children Play," 274.
5. Malcolm Gay, May 7, 2017. "Peabody Essex Museum Hires Neuroscientist to Enhance Visitor Experience" *Boston Globe* http://www.bostonglobe.com/arts/art/2017/05/07/peabody-essex-museum-hires-neuroscientist-enhance-visitor-experience/MmyHmYXUWvAUEb058PPJNO/story.html?s_campaign=8315. Quote from Dan Monroe, the museum's director and CEO.
6. Mihalyi Csikszentmihalyi, 1991. "Notes on Art Museum Experiences." In Getty Center for Education in the Arts and J. Paul Getty Museum, *Insights: Museums, Visitors, Attitudes, Expectations: A Focus Group Experiment*, Malibu, CA: J. Paul Getty Trust, 123–31.

Chapter 1

1. Nina Simon, Wednesday, November 20, 2013. *Let's Stop Talking About What People Want and Need as If They Are Different (And We Can Tell How)*. Museum 2.0. http://museumtwo.blogspot.com/2013/11/lets-stop-talking-about-what-people-need.html.
2. National Center on Universal Design for Learning. http://www.udlcenter.org/aboutudl/whatisudl.
3. Teaching Literacy Through Art, 2002–2006, funded by a grant from the U.S. Department of Education and conducted in partnership with Randi Korn and Associates. https://www.guggenheim.org/education-research-studies

Chapter 2

1. Anonymous written evaluation, personal communication, July 17, 2015.
2. Sharon Vatsky, "Connecting Collections: Integrating Modern and Contemporary Art into the Classroom," in *Professional Development in Art Museums: Strategies of Engagement Through, Contemporary Art,*

eds. Dana Carlisle Kletchka B. and Stephen Carpenter, II, (Reston, VA: National Art Education Association, 2017).
3. See Connecting Collections Teacher Institute on Facebook
4. See Appendix 1, Lesson Plan Template.

Chapter 3

1. Charles C. Bonwell and James A. Eison, 1991. *Active Learning: Creating Excitement in the Classroom.* 2. Association for the Study of Higher Education. Washington, DC: George Washington University School of Education and Human Development.
2. University of Minnesota, Center for Educational Innovation. https://cei.umn.edu/support-services/tutorials/what-active-learning
3. John H. Falk and Lynn D. Dierking, *Learning from Museums: Visitor Experiences and the Making of Meaning* (Walnut Creek, CA: AltaMira Press, 2000), 203.
4. *Creating the Future Perspectives on Educational Change.* Compiled and edited by Dee Dickinson. Intelligence in Seven Steps, Howard Gardner, Ph.D. http://education.jhu.edu/PD/newhorizons/future/creating_the_future/crfut_gardner.cfm
5. George E. Hein, *Learning in the Museum* (London and New York: Routledge, 1998).
6. George E. Hein, *The Constructivist Museum* (1995), http://www.gem.org.uk/pubs/news/hein1995.php
7. Daniela Fenker and Harmut Schütze, December 17, 2008. "Learning by Surprise," Scientific American https://www.scientificamerican.com/article/learning-by-surprise/
8. Donald J. Ford, July 20, 2011, *How the Brain Learns,* https://www.trainingindustry.com/content-development/articles/how-the-brain-learns.aspx

Chapter 4

1. Goodreads. Albert Einstein quotes, http://www.goodreads.com/quotes/133135-learning-is-experience-everything-else-is-just-information
2. Elijah Freiman, March 6, 2014, *The Socratic Method—The New but Old Way to Teach and Learn.* Teach to Learn Foundation. http://teach2learnfoundation.org/2014/03/06/socratic-method-teach-learn/
3. Judy Rand, "The 227-Mile Museum or a Visitor's Bill of Rights," *Curator: The Museum Journal* 44, no.1 (January 2000): 7–14. http://www.informalscience.org/227-mile-museum-or-why-we-need-visitors-bill-rights.
4. Abraham H. Maslow, "A Theory of Human Motivation," *Psychological Review* 50, no. 4 (July 1943): 370–96, https://docs.google.com/file/d/0B-5-JeCa2Z7hNjZlNDNhOTEtMWNkYi00YmFhLWI3Y-jUtMDEyMDJkZDExNWRm/edit
5. This tip courtesy of Guggenheim educator, Missy Lipsett.
6. Catherine Egenberger and Philip Yenawine. 2001. *As Theory Becomes Practice: The Happy Tale of a School/Museum Partnership.* http://vtshome.org/wp-content/uploads/2016/08/13As-Theory-Becomes-Practice-.pdf, 6–7.
7. See Portable Seats/Folding Stools for Museum Guests. http://community.aam-us.org/communities/community-home/digestviewer/viewthread?MessageKey=87ad7064-0645-4f8b-af3d-39a71a957f48&CommunityKey=d34b2dfb-4151-4629-a59a-553d0ae428d9&tab=digestviewer&UserKey=fdabefd6-a9e8-47a9-951c7d28d70e7141&sKey=3c5aac5438f34bb881d3#bm87ad7064-0645-4f8b-af3d-39a71a957f48
8. Benjamin Ives Gilman, "Museum Fatigue," *The Scientific Monthly* 2, no. 1 (1916): 62–74.
9. Personal conversation with a tour participant, July 2017.
10. Model Magic® is a nontoxic modeling material that dries within twenty-four to thirty-six hours without kiln firing. It is manufactured and distributed by Crayola®. http://www.crayola.com/
11. Self-Adhesive Laminating Sheets are a product of Avery Dennison Corporation. www.avery.com
12. Chip Wood, 2007. *Yardsticks: Children in the Classroom Ages 4–14*, 3rd edition (Turners Falls, MA: Northeast Foundation for Children, 2007).
13. *AAC and Autism: Using Communication Devices for Non-Verbal Children.* Speech and Language Kids. https://www.speechandlanguagekids.com/giving-voice-non-verbal-children-autism-aac-autism/

14. National Association of the Deaf. https://www.nad.org/resources/technology/assistive-listening/assistive-listening-systems-and-devices/
15. Margarita Tartakovsky, *The Importance of Play for Adults*, Psych Central. *https://psychcentral.com/blog/archives/2012/11/15/the-importance-of-play-for-adults/*
16. Rachel Ropeik. 2014. *Long Live the Spirit of Play: Tracking a Theme Through NAEA 2014.* (National Art Education Association) https://artmuseumteaching.com/2014/04/18/spirit-of-play/

Chapter 5

1. http://www.goodreads.com/quotes/264509-i-don-t-know-what-i-think-until-i-write-it
2. http://www.goodreads.com/quotes/315733-i-write-because-i-don-t-know-what-i-think-until
3. Saltz and Irving Sandler. September 12, 2008. *The Brooklyn Rail*, http://brooklynrail.org/2008/09/art/jerry-saltz-in-conversation-with-irving-sandler
4. Camille Pissarro, *The Hermitage at Pontoise*, ca. 1867, Oil on canvas, 59 5/8 x 79 inches (151.4 x 200.6 cm), Solomon R. Guggenheim Museum, New York Thannhauser Collection, Gift, Justin K. Thannhauser, 1978, https://www.guggenheim.org/artwork/3465
5. Teaching Literacy Through Art, 2002–2006, funded by a grant from the U.S. Department of Education and conducted in partnership with Randi Korn and Associates. https://www.guggenheim.org/education-research-studies.
6. See the appendix for an activity sheet.
7. Be sure that your museum's curatorial and conservation departments approve these for use in the galleries.
8. https://www.poets.org/poetsorg/text/play-exquisite-corpse
9. https://www.guggenheim.org/artwork/3699 accessed 5/5/2017
10. http://www.dictionary.com/browse/cinquain
11. Susan Sollins, "Games Children Play in Museums," *Art Journal* (spring 1971): 274.
12. Constanin Brancusi (1876–1957) *Little French Girl (The First Step [III])*, ca. 1914–1918 (mounted by museum, 1953, oak on pine base, figure: 49 x 9 3/8 x 9 1/4 inches (124.5 x 23.8 x 23.5 cm); base: 11 x 15 1/4 x 13 inches (27.9 x 38.7 x 33 cm), Solomon R. Guggenheim Museum, New York, Gift, Estate of Katherine S. Dreier, 1953, https://www.guggenheim.org/artwork/661
13. I first saw this activity facilitated by Susan McCullough, a former museum educator teacher programs at the Museum of Modern Art, who now teaches in the education department at the City College of New York.
14. Harvard Graduate School of Education. http://www.pz.harvard.edu/.
15. Visible thinking, http://www.visiblethinkingpz.org/VisibleThinking_html_files/VisibleThinking1.html
16. http://www.visiblethinkingpz.org/VisibleThinking_html_files/03_ThinkingRoutines/03c_Core_routines/SeeThinkWonder/SeeThinkWonder_Routine.html
17. Ron Ritchart, Mark Church, and Karen Morrison, *Making Thinking Visible: How to Promote Engagement, Understanding, and Independence for All Learners* (San Francisco: Jossey-Bass, 2011): 56–57.
18. http://www.visiblethinkingpz.org/VisibleThinking_html_files/03_ThinkingRoutines/03c_Core_routines/UsedToThink/UsedToThink_Routine.htm
19. Ritchart, Church, and Morrison, *Making Thinking Visible*, 154–61.
20. Merriam Webster dictionary, https://www.merriam-webster.com/dictionary/manifesto
21. F. T. Marinetti, "The Founding and Manifesto of Futurism" (excerpt) in *Futurism: An Anthology*, eds. Lawrence Rainey, Christine Poggi, and Laura Wittman (New Haven, CT: Yale University Press, 2009) https://modernistarchitecture.files.wordpress.com/2011/09/ebooksclub-org__futurism__an_anthology__henry_mcbride_series_in_modernism_.pdf
22. Grammarly. 07/11/2014 09:10 am ET | Updated Sep 10, 2014. "How To Write Your Manifesto in 5 Steps" http://www.huffingtonpost.com/grammarly/write-manifesto_b_5575496.html
23. Art Beyond Sight. http://www.artbeyondsight.org/handbook/acs-guidelines.shtml

Chapter 6

1. Betty Edwards, *Drawing on the Right Side of the Brain* (Los Angeles: J. P. Tarcher, 1979), 87.
2. Kimon Nicolaides, *The Natural Way to Draw* (Boston, MA: Houghton Mifflin, 1941), xiii.

3. Nancy Smith and the Drawing Study Group. *Observation Drawing with Children: A Framework for Teachers*. p.12. New York, NY: Teachers College Press.

4. Rika Burnham, head of education, Frick Collection, NY.

5. Paul Cézanne (1839–1906), *Still Life: Plate of Peaches* 1879–1880. Oil on canvas, 23 1/2 x 28 7/8 inches (59.7 x 73.3 cm), https://www.guggenheim.org/artwork/782

6. Carey Dunne. November 24, 2015. "Rijksmuseum Asks Visitors to Stop Taking Photos and Start Sketching the Art." Hyperallergic. https://hyperallergic.com/256575/rijksmuseum-asks-visitors-to -stop-taking-photos-and-start-sketching-the-art/.

7. Ibid.

8. Prismacolor Art Stix®. http://www.prismacolor.com/products/colored-pencils/art-stix

9. Dick Blick. http://www.dickblick.com/products/blick-sketch-pad-boards/?clickTracking=true& wmcp=pla&wmcid=items&wmckw=22945-1007&gclid=CNDGwc-p5NMCFRIXDQodysgDQg

10. See discussion of gallery stools in chapter 4, "Guidelines for Creating Gallery Activities."

11. Merriam-Webster Dictionary. https://www.merriam-webster.com/dictionary/viewfinder

12. Gepe 2x2 Standard 35mm Slide Mounts (24x36), Glassless, Pack of 100, https://www.adorama.com/ gp7001.html

13. Hiufu Wong, Sunday, April 13, 2014, "Most photographed places in the world are . . ." CNN. http:// www.cnn.com/2014/04/13/travel/photo-map-popular-cities/

14. Poets.org. https://www.poets.org/poetsorg/text/play-exquisite-corpse

15. Sharon Vatsky. 2002. Guggenheim Museum, The Curriculum Online. https://www.guggenheim.org/ arts-curriculum/topic/vasily-kandinsky-composition-8

16. Pablo Picasso (1881–1973) Collection Online. Solomon R. Guggenheim Museum. New York. https:// www.guggenheim.org/artwork/3426

17. Jan Avikos, Collection Online. Solomon R. Guggenheim Museum. New York. https://www .guggenheim.org/artwork/3426

18. Pablo Picasso (1881–1973), Collection Online. Solomon R. Guggenheim Museum. New York. https:// www.guggenheim.org/artwork/3427

19. The early phase of Cubism is characterized by the use of multiple viewpoints, overlapping planes, and monochromatic color.

20. Qiu Zhijie. 2017 *Map of the Theater of the World*. Ink on paper mounted to silk six panels, 94 1/2 inches x 23 feet 7 7/16 inches (240 x 720 cm) overall. Solomon R. Guggenheim Museum, New York, Gift of the artist with additional funds contributed by the International Director's Council, 2017 2017.48 https:// www.guggenheim.org/artwork/36123

21. Qiu Zhijie. *Art and China after 1989: Theater of the World.* https://www.guggenheim.org/arts-curriculum/topic/qiu-zhijie.

22. Luis Camnitzer, 2014, *Teachers Guide, Under the Same Sun*. Solomon R. Guggenheim Museum. https://www.guggenheim.org/wp-content/uploads/2016/03/guggenheim-map-under-the-same -sun-teachers-guide-english-luis-camnitzer.pdf

23. Franz Marc (1880–1916). Collection online. https://www.guggenheim.org/artwork/artist/franz-marc

24. Franz Marc (1880–1916). *The Unfortunate Land of Tyrol*, 1913, Oil on canvas, 4 feet 3 5/8 inches x 6 feet 6 3/4 inches. Solomon R. Guggenheim Museum, New York: Solomon R. Guggenheim Founding Collection. https://www.guggenheim.org/artwork/artist/franz-marc

25. This activity is adapted from Robert Kaupelis, *Experimental Drawing* (New York: Watson-Guptill, 1980): 54–55.

Chapter 7

1. Lygia Clark, *Time*, November 22, 1968, Volume 92, Part 2, 77. https://books.google.com/books?id=6_geA-QAAMAAJ&q=%E2%80%9CWe+do+everything+so+automatically+77+Lygia+Clark&dq=%E2%80%9CWe+do+everything+so+automatically+77+Lygia+Clark&hl=en&sa=X&ved=0ahUKEwjfnsaD3Y7VAhUSID4KHZcxBcwQ6AEIJDAA. http://www.art-quotes.com/getquotes.php?catid=275#.WVB2lo7ysdU

2. Pablo Picasso, 1904. *Woman Ironing*. Oil on canvas, 45 3/4 x 28 3/4 inches (116.2 x 73 cm), Solomon R. Guggenheim Museum, NY. https://www.guggenheim.org/artwork/3417

3. Pierre-Auguste Renoir, 1871. *Woman with Parakeet.* Oil on canvas, 36 1/4 x 25 5/8 inches (92.1 x 65.1 cm) Solomon R. Guggenheim Museum, NY. https://www.guggenheim.org/artwork/3699

4. Joan Mitchell, 1969. *Sunflower.* Oil on canvas, 102 x 70 1/2 in. (259.1 x 179.1 cm) Metropolitan Museum of Art, NY. http://www.metmuseum.org/art/collection/search/485308

5. Antonio de Pereda, 1634. *Still Life with Walnuts.* Oil on canvas, diameter: 8 1/8 inches (20.7 cm), Joaquín Achúcarro, Madrid, Spain. https://www.flickr.com/photos/eoskins/11936471046

6. Jackson Pollock, 1947. *Alchemy.* Oil, aluminum, alkyd enamel paint with sand, pebbles, fibers, and wood on commercially printed fabric, 45 1/8 x 87 1/8 inches (114.6 x 221.3 cm), The Solomon R. Guggenheim Foundation, Peggy Guggenheim Collection, Venice. https://www.guggenheim.org/artwork/3482

7. Khadim Ali, https://www.guggenheim.org/artwork/artist/khadim-ali

8. Soheap Pich, 2011. *Morning Glory.* Rattan, bamboo, wire, plywood, and steel, 74 inches x 103 inches x 17 feet 6 inches (188 x 261.6 x 533.4 cm). Solomon R. Guggenheim Museum, NY. https://www.guggenheim.org/artwork/artist/sopheap-pich

9. "Peter Fischli David Weiss: How to Work Better." February 5–April 27, 2016, Solomon R. Guggenheim Museum, NY, https://www.guggenheim.org/exhibition/peter-fischli-david-weiss-how-to-work-better

10. Julie Belcove, "Shelf Life." May 23, 2016, *The New Yorker.* http://www.newyorker.com/magazine/2016/05/23/kader-attias-couscous-architecture-in-the-guggenheim

11. Rachel Whiteread. 2001.*Untitled (Basement).* White robust plasticized plaster, 10 feet 8 inches x 21 feet 7 inches x 12 feet 1 inches (325.1 x 657.9 x 368.3 cm), Solomon R. Guggenheim Museum, New York Commissioned by Deutsche Bank AG in consultation with the Solomon R. Guggenheim Foundation for the Deutsche Guggenheim, Berlin 2005.119 © Rachel Whiteread. https://www.guggenheim.org/artwork/10836

12. Alberto Burri, http://exhibitions.guggenheim.org/burri/art/sacks/sacco-sf-1-1954

13. Caitlin Hayes, "Learning, Memory and the Sense of Smell." https://research.cornell.edu/news-features/learning-memory-and-sense-smell

14. Anicka Yi, The Hugo Boss Prize 2016: "Life Is Cheap." https://www.guggenheim.org/exhibition/the-hugo-boss-prize-2016

15. Pieter Brugel the Elder, 1567. "The Peasant Wedding" Oil on panel, 114 cm × 164 cm (45 in × 65 in). Kunsthistorisches Museum, Vienna. https://en.wikipedia.org/wiki/Pieter_Bruegel_the_Elder

16. Carmen Papalia.com. https://carmenpapalia.com/about/

17. Carmen Papalia, 2014. "The Touchy Subject." Solomon R. Guggenheim Museum, NY. https://www.guggenheim.org/video/the-touchy-subject

18. Jordan Gaines Lewis, January 12, 2015. "Smells Ring Bells: How Smell Triggers Memories and Emotions." *Psychology Today.* https://www.psychologytoday.com/blog/brain-babble/201501/smells-ring-bells-how-smell-triggers-memories-and-emotions

Chapter 8

1. http://dedalusfoundation.org/robert-motherwell-early-collages-guggenheim

2. Avery® Self-Adhesive Laminating Sheets 73601, 9" x 12", box of fifty. Product number 73601.

3. Hygloss Collage Sticky Boards, https://www.dickblick.com/products/hygloss-collage-sticky-boards/#photos

4. Wikki Stix website. https://www.wikkistix.com/

5. *David Smith: A Centennial*, February 3–May 14, 2006, Solomon R. Guggenheim Museum. https://www.guggenheim.org/arts-curriculum/resource-unit/david-smith-a-centennial

6. *Hudson River Landscape*, 1951. Welded steel, 125.7 x 190.5 x 42.5 cm. Whitney Museum of American Art, New York. © Estate of David Smith / Licensed by VAGA, New York, NY

7. Albany and Poughkeepsie are two cities in New York State that are adjacent to the Hudson River.

8. Tang Da Wu. 2012. *Our Children.* Galvanized steel, glass, and milk; three parts: 62 x 89 ½ x 23 ½ , 26 ¼ x 44 ½ x 12, and 8 ½ x 3/1/8 inches. Overall dimensions vary with installation. Solomon R. Guggenheim Museum, New York, Guggenheim UBS Purchase Fund, 2012. © Tang Da Wu. https://www.guggenheim.org/arts-curriculum/topic/tang-da-wu

9. Beate Söntgen, 2005. "Peter Fischli and David Weiss: In Conversation, January 2004, Zürich," in Press-PLAY. London: Phaidon. 192.
10. Model Magic® is a nontoxic modeling material that dries within twenty-four to thirty-six hours without kiln firing. It is manufactured and distributed by Crayola®. http://www.crayola.com/
11. Sharon Vatsky, 2003. *The Architecture of the Solomon R. Guggenheim Museum.* https://www.guggenheim.org/arts-curriculum/topic/geometric-shapes#_edn2
12. Email communication with Cari Frisch, associate educator, family programs, Museum of Modern Art, Wednesday, October 12, 2017.
13. https://www.artsy.net/gene/color-field-painting
14. You can just lay the color chips on top of the white cardstock or with a matte knife, make two parallel 8" horizontal slits about 2" apart leaving a 2" border on the left and right , so that you can tuck the edges of the color chips into the slits on the cardstock.
15. Marden, Brice. Collection Online, Solomon R. Guggenheim Museum. .https://www.guggenheim.org/artwork/artist/brice-marden
16. Morris Louis, Collection Online, Solomon R. Guggenheim Museum. https://www.guggenheim.org/artwork/artist/morris-louis
17. Kenneth Noland, Collection Online, Solomon R. Guggenheim Museum. https://www.guggenheim.org/artwork/artist/kenneth-noland

Chapter 9

1. Viola Spolin, *Los Angeles Times.* May 26, 1974.
2. Shannon Murphy, December 6, 2012. "Tableaux Vivant: History and Practice, Art Museum Teaching." https://artmuseumteaching.com/2012/12/06/tableaux-vivant-history-and-practice/
3. Ibid.
4. Bernard Friedberg, 1972. *Arts Awareness: A Project of the Metropolitan Museum of Art.* New York. http://libmma.contentdm.oclc.org/cdm/ref/collection/p15324coll10/id/185526
5. Susan Sollins, "Games Children Play: In Museums," *Art Journal*, New York: College Art Association (spring 1972): 271–75.
6. Ibid., 274.
7. Frank Sinatra School of the Arts, Queens, NY http://franksinatraschoolofthearts.org/
8. See Circle through New York. https://www.circlethroughnewyork.com/things-1/#/high-school-drama-class/
9. *Sunday in the Park with George.* https://en.wikipedia.org/wiki/Sunday_in_the_Park_with_George
10. *Victory of Samothrace.* c.190 B.C. Marble, height 96". The Louvre, Paris.
11. Eugéne Delacroix, *Liberty Guiding the People*.1830. Oil on canvas. 2.6 x 3.25m. The Louvre, Paris.
12. Johannes Vermeer, *Young Woman with a Water Jug.* ca. 1662. oil on canvas; 18 x 16 in. (45.7 x 40.6 cm.) The Metropolitan Museum of Art, New York.
13. https://www.merriam-webster.com/dictionary/mindfulness
14. Shannon Murphy. 2016. Chapter 7, "Engaging with Silence: Using Art as a Heuristic to Develop Understanding About Meditation." In: M. Powietrzynska and K. Tobin (eds). *Mindfulness and Educating Citizens for Everyday Life.* Bold Visions in Educational Research. SensePublishers, Rotterdam. 107.
15. For a fuller discussion of using mindfulness as a productive museum education strategy, see Shannon Murphy's article cited above.

Chapter 10

1. Vasily Kandinsky, *Concerning the Spiritual in Art*, Munich, 1912. 42 (original). https://www.guggenheim.org/arts-curriculum/topic/vasily-kandinsky-composition-8#_edn4, or Wassily Kandinsky, *Concerning the Spiritual in Art*, 1977. M. T. H. Sadler, translator, New York: Dover Publications, p. 29. (The Dover edition is an unabridged republication of the English translation first published by Constable and Company Ltd., London, 1914, under the title *The Art of Spiritual Harmony*.)

2. http://petermedhurst.com/study-days/music-inspired-by-paintings/
3. Two companies producing CDs that focus on the relationship between music and art are Museum Music http://museummusic.com and Naxos Records https://www.naxos.com
4. https://en.wikipedia.org/wiki/Chromesthesia
5. Clement Jewitt, July 2000. *Music at the Bauhaus, 1919–1933*. Tempo, New Series, No. 213, p. 6. University Press. http://www.jstor.org/stable/946540
6. http://bensidran.com/writing/the-jazz-of-stuart-davis
7. Jackson Pollock Jazz. http://Museummusic.Com/Jacksonpollockjazz.Aspx
8. Carlos Amorales, (b. 1970). *We'll See How Everything Reverberates*, 2012. Copper alloy, steel, and epoxy paint three parts: one part 23 feet (700 cm) diameter; two parts, 16 feet 5 inches (500 cm) diameter; 16 feet 5 inches (500 cm) diameter. Solomon R. Guggenheim Museum, New York Guggenheim UBS MAP Purchase Fund, 2014. 2014.7. © Carlos Amorales https://www.guggenheim.org/artwork/33019

Chapter 11

1. Adam Gopnik, June 12, 2007. *The Mindful Museum*, The Walrus. https://thewalrus.ca/the-mindful-museum/#.WeKmr3E9YbE.email.
2. Gary Tinterow, "The Blockbuster, Art History, and the Public," in *The Two Art Histories: The Museum and the University*, edited by Charles Haxthausen (Williamstown, MA: Sterling and Francine Clark Art Institute, 2002): 151.
3. Ben Tappin, Leslie Van Der Leer, and Ryan McKay. May 27, 2017. "You're Not Going to Change Your Mind," *The New York Times Sunday Review*, https://www.nytimes.com/2017/05/27/opinion/sunday/youre-not-going-to-change-your-mind.html?emc=eta1.
4. David Bowles is a museum educator formerly at the Metropolitan Museum of Art and currently at the J. Paul Getty Museum.
5. Georges Seurat (1859–1891). *Circus Sideshow*. 1887–88, Oil on canvas, 39 1/4 x 59 in. (99.7 x 149.9 cm).The Metropolitan Museum of Art. http://www.metmuseum.org/toah/works-of-art/61.101.17/.
6. Annette Labedzki. December 30, 2009. *Divisionism–An Unusual Painting Technique.* http://ezinearticles.com/?Divisionism–An-Unusual-Painting-Technique&id=3498375. This quote also appears at the top of the Met Museum worksheet distributed during tour.
7. Jane King Hession and Debra Pickrel, Frank Lloyd Wright in New York: The Plaza Years, 1954-1959 (Layton, UT: Gibbs Smith, 2017): 113.
8. John Hutchinson, March 14, 2016. *Infographic Reveals The World's Most Photographed Tourist Attractions.* Daily Mail.com. http://www.dailymail.co.uk/travel/travel_news/article-3487587/Infographic-reveals-world-s-photographed-tourist-attractions-Eiffel-Tower-doesn-t-make-list.html.
9. Megan Kuensting is a museum educator at the Metropolitan Museum of Art.
10. Mark Tansey (1949–). 1981. *The Innocent Eye Test.* Oil on canvas, 78 x 120 in. (198.1 x 304.8 cm) The Metropolitan Museum of Art. http://www.metmuseum.org/art/collection/search/48497.
11. Amelia Gentlemen, October 19, 2004. "Smile Please." *The Guardian.* https://www.theguardian.com/artanddesign/2004/oct/19/art.france.
12. Thomas Hart Benton (1889–1975). *America Today.* 1930–31. Ten panels: Egg tempera with oil glazing over Permalba on a gesso ground on linen mounted to wood panels with a honeycomb interior, The Metropolitan Museum of Art. http://www.metmuseum.org/toah/works-of-art/2012.478a-j/.
13. Claire Moore is a museum educator formerly at the Metropolitan Museum of Art and currently education director at the Dallas Museum of Art.
14. Hollie Ecker and Sarah Mostow are experienced museum educators and teaching artists.
15. Emily Rivlin-Nadler, *Visionaries: Creating a Modern Guggenheim, Family Guide.* https://www.guggenheim.org/wp-content/uploads/2016/07/guggenheim-exhibitions-visionaries-family-activity-guide-2.10.17.pdf
16. Princeton Art Museum. http://artmuseum.princeton.edu/cezanne-modern/c%C3%A9zanne/mont-sainte-victoire.
17. National Council on Public History http://ncph.org/phc/ncph-working-groups/museums-civic-discourse-2016-working-group/

Chapter 12

1. This chapter is written in collaboration with Rebecca Mir, former associate manager, digital media and online learning at the Solomon R. Guggenheim Museum.
2. Teachbytes. March 3, 2012. https://teachbytes.com/2012/03/01/10-educational-technology -quotes/.
3. Mike Murawski, July 6, 2013. *Un/Plugged: Are We Becoming Too Reliant on Technology?* https://art museumteaching.com/2013/07/06/museums-unplugged/
4. Kristin Thomson, Kristen Purcell, and Lee Rainie, January 4, 2013. *Arts Organizations and Digital Technologies.* The Pew Research Center's Internet & American Life Project. http://www.pewinternet .org/2013/01/04/arts-organizations-and-digital-technologies/
5. Ibid.
6. Murawski, *Un/Plugged: Are We Becoming Too Reliant on Technology?*
7. *Engage: The Future of Museums. Interim Findings from Roundtable Discussions on Audience Engagement and the Role of the Museum in the Community.* 2014. San Francisco, California: Gensler. https://www .gensler.com/uploads/document/395/file/gensler_museum-research-interim-report.pdf. P.18.
8. Ai Wee Seow is currently program director at STAR, Singapore, a professional development facility dedicated to improving the quality of art and music education. https://www.facebook.com/pg/ STARSingapore/about/?ref=page_internal
9. Andy Warhol (1928–1987). *Dance Diagram, 5 (Fox Trot: "The Right Turn—Man")*, 1962. Casein, graphite pencil, and masking tape on canvas, Overall: 83 1/4 × 24 5/16 in. (211.5 × 61.8 cm). Whitney Museum of American Art, New York; Gift of The American Contemporary Art Foundation, Inc., Leonard A. Lauder, President. © Andy Warhol Foundation for the Visual Arts/Artists Rights Society (ARS), New York. http://collection.whitney.org/object/17218.
10. National History Education Clearinghouse. http://teachinghistory.org/digital-classroom/tech-for -teachers/24636.
11. Susan Sontag, *On Photography* (New York: Farrar, Straus & Giroux, 1973): 18.
12. Brian X. Chen, July 20, 2016. "What's the Right Age for a Child to Get a Smartphone?" *New York Times.* https://www.nytimes.com/2016/07/21/technology/personaltech/whats-the-right-age-to-give-a -child-a-smartphone.html.
13. Linda A. Henkel, December 5, 2013. *Point-and-Shoot Memories The Influence of Taking Photos on Memory for a Museum Tour* I http://journals.sagepub.com/doi/abs/10.1177/0956797613504438
14. Megan Gannon, December 9, 2013, 01:19 pm ET. "Want to Remember Your Museum Visit? Don't Take Pictures." *Live Science.* https://www.livescience.com/41803-snapping-photos-museum-memories .html.
15. We have used the following applications: doodles! Express, Appikiko LLC; Paper Express, miSofware; Action Painting Lite, SungLab.
16. Informal observations by teaching artist Jeff Hopkins, working with sixth grade students at Public School 86, Bronx, NY in Learning Through Art, a program of the Guggenheim Museum. 2014.
17. Carey Dunne, November 24, 2015. "Rijksmuseum Asks Visitors to Stop Taking Photos and Start Sketching the Art." Hyperallergic. https://hyperallergic.com/256575/rijksmuseum-asks-visitors-to -stop-taking-photos-and-start-sketching-the-art/

Chapter 13

1. Ben Shahn, *The Shape of Content* (New York: Vintage Books, 1960): 45.
2. Alejandro Cesarco. (1975–). *Index.* 2000. 12 chromogenic prints. 20 x 16 inches (50 x 40.6 cm) each Solomon R. Guggenheim Museum, New York Guggenheim UBS MAP Purchase Fund, 2014.
3. Alejandro Cesarco's *Index* can be read in its entirety at Tanya Leighton Gallery, Berlin, Germany. http:// www.tanyaleighton.com/index.php?pageId=233&l=en
4. Ibid.
5. Alexandra Munroe and Ming Tiampo. 2013. *Gutai: Splendid Playground.* New York: Guggenheim Museum.

6. To see an image from this performance, see Ellen Pearlman. March 18, 2013. The Alchemical Art Innovators of Postwar Japan. https://hyperallergic.com/66520/the-alchemical-art-innovators-of-post war-japan/.

7. Queena Ko is a museum educator and teaching artist who works at the Guggenheim and other New York City museums.

8. Saburō Murakami. *Speed Violation.* Alexandra Munroe and Ming Tiampo. 2013. *Gutai: Splendid Playground.* New York: Guggenheim Museum. 278. Excerpt. Originally published as "E no koto: Supīdo ihan" [About pictures: Speed violation], Kirin (April 1961), 20–21.

9. Antonio de Pereda (1611–1678). *Vanitas.* ca.1660. Oil on canvas.13 x15.6 inches (33 x 39.5 cm). Museo De Zaragoza, Spain. http://www.museodezaragoza.es/colecciones/barroco/. and at http://web .guggenheim.org/exhibitions/picasso/artworks/skull.

10. *Spanish Painting from El Greco to Picasso: Time, Truth and History.* November 17, 2006–March 28, 2007. Gimenéz Carmen and Francisco Calvo Serraller curators. Solomon R. Guggenheim Museum.

11. Sharon Vatsky, *Spanish Painting from El Greco to Picasso: Time, Truth and History.* Teacher Guide (New York: Solomon R. Guggenheim Museum, 2006): 45. https://www.guggenheim.org/wp-content/uploads/2016/09/guggenheim-education-spanish-paining-from-el-greco-to-picasso-resource-unit.pdf

12. Christopher Wool (1955–), *Black Book Drawings*, 1989. Enamel on paper (suite of 22 drawings) 40" x 26" each. https://www.guggenheim.org/exhibition/christopher-wool.

13. Christopher Wool, Teacher Resource Unit. https://www.guggenheim.org/arts-curriculum/resource-unit/christopher-wool.

14. Gabriel Orozco (1962–). *Astroturf Constellation,* 2012, 1,188 found objects, including plastic, glass, paper, metal, and other materials, dimensions variable Solomon R. Guggenheim Museum, New York Commissioned by Deutsche Bank AG in consultation with the Solomon R. Guggenheim Foundation for the Deutsche Guggenheim, Berlin https://www.guggenheim.org/artwork/30592

Appendix 1

1. This template was developed collaboratively with members of the education departments at the Metropolitan Museum of Art, the Museum of Modern Art, the Whitney Museum of American Art, and the Solomon R. Guggenheim Museum for distribution during an annual weeklong professional development institute, *Connecting Collections: Integrating Modern and Contemporary Art into the Classroom.*

2. An advance organizer is a tool used to introduce a new tour theme and highlight the relationship between what the tour participants are about to learn and the information they already know, so that the new information can be remembered more easily. They remind participants that they already have a storehouse of information pertaining to the theme that will be explored on the tour. http://study.com/academy/lesson/advanced-organizers-in-the-classroom-teaching-strategies-advantages.html.

3. Group reflection: An opportunity to look back on the tour experience. There are many ways to build in reflection into tours, but the goals of a reflection include considering what the group accomplished and learned and sharing ideas and responses with others in the group.

Appendix 2

1. Wassily Kandinsky, *Concerning the Spiritual in Art*, 1977. M. T. H. Sadler, translator, New York: Dover Publications, 29. (The Dover edition is an unabridged republication of the English translation first published by Constable and Company Ltd., London, 1914, under the title *The Art of Spiritual Harmony.*)

Bibliography

Armstrong, Thomas. *Multiple Intelligences in the Classroom*, Third Edition. ASCD: Alexandria, VA, 2009.

Art Museum Teaching: A forum for reflecting n practice, https://artmuseumteaching.com

Burnham, Rika. Summer. "If You Don't Stop, You Don't See Anything," *Teachers College Record* 95 (1994): 520–35.

Burnham, Rika, and Elliot Kai Kee. "The Art of Teaching in the Museum," *Journal of Aesthetic Education* 39, no. 1 (Spring 2007): 65-76.

Burnham, Rika, and Elliot Kai-Kee. *Teaching in the Art Museum: Interpretation as Experience.* Los Angeles CA: J. Paul Getty Museum, 2011.

Csikszentmihaliy, Mihaly. "Intrinsic Motivation in Museums: Why Does One Want to Learn?" in *The Educational Role of the Museum: Second Edition.* New York: Routledge, 2001.

Ehrenworth, Mary. *Looking to Write: Children Writing Through the Visual Arts.* Teachers College Reading and Writing Project, Columbia University, Heinemann, Portsmouth, NH, 2003.

Fagin, Larry. *The List Poem: A Guide to Teaching and Writing Catalog Verse.* New York: Teachers & Writers Collaborative, 1991 (2000).

Falk, John H., and Lynn D. Dierking. *Learning from Museums: Visitor Experiences and the Making of Meaning.* Walnut Creek CA: AltaMira Press, 2000.

Falk, John H., and Lynn D. Dierking. *The Museum Experience Revisited.* Walnut Creek, CA: Left Coast Press, 2013.

Foster, Tonya, and Kristin Prevallet. *Third Mind: Creative Writing through Visual Art.* New York: Teachers & Writers Collaborative, 2002.

Gardner, Howard. *Frames of Mind: The Theory of Multiple Intelligences.* New York: Basic Books, 1983.

Gardner, Howard, 2012. *In a Nutshell,* https://howardgardner01.files.wordpress.com/2012/06/in-a-nutshell-minh.pdf

Greenhill, Eilean Hooper. "Learning in Art Museums: Strategies of Interpretation" in *The Educational Role of the Museum: Second Edition,* edited by Eilean Hooper Greenhill, 44–52. New York: Routledge, 2001.

Hein, George. *Learning in the Museum.* New York: Routledge, 1998.

Hein, George. "Is Meaning Making Constructivism? Is Constructivism Meaning Making?" *The Exhibitionist* 18(2): 15–18. http://www.george-hein.com/downloads/Hein_isMeaningMaking.pdf

Hein, George. "The Constructivist Museum," in *The Educational Role of the Museum*: Second Edition. New York: Routledge, 2001.

Hein, George. "John Dewey and Museum Education," *Curator: The Museum Journal* 47 no. 4: 413–27. http://www.george-hein.com/downloads/Hein_DeweyMuseumEd.pdf

Hubard, Olga. "What Does Constructivism Have to Do with My Classroom?" *Activities in the Art Museum, NAEA Advisory* (Fall 2006): 1–2. Thirteen Ed online. Http://www.thirteen.org/edonline/concept2class/constructivism/index_sub2.html

Hubard, Olga. 2007. "Productive Information: Contextual Knowledge in Art Museum Education," *Art Education* 60 no. 4 (2007): 17–23.

Hubard, Olga. "Complete Engagement: Embodied Response in Art Museum Education." *Art Education* 60 no. 6 (2007): 46–53.

Hubard, Olga. April 14, 2014. *In the Midst of Practice: Reflections on Gallery Teachings Marathon,* in Art Museum Teaching, http://artmuseumteaching.com/2014/04/14/in-the-midst-of-practice/

Hubard, Olga. 2015. "Engagement: Embodied Response and Multimodal Facilitation" in *Art Museum Education: Facilitating Gallery Experiences,* 1st ed. London: Palgrave Macmillan, 2015.

Jackson, Philip W. *John Dewey and the Lessons of Art.* New Haven, CT: Yale University Press, 1998.

Jensen, Eric. *Arts with the Brain in Mind.* Alexandria, VA: Association for Supervision and Curriculum Development, 2001.

Levent, Nina, and Alvaro Pascual-Leone. *The Multisensory Museum: Cross-Disciplinary Perspectives on Touch, Sound, Smell, Memory, and Space.* Lanham MD: Rowman and Littlefield, 2014.

Mayer, M. M. "Scintillating Conversations." In *Periphery to Center: Art Museum Education in the 21st Century,* edited by P. Villeneuve, 188–93. Reston, VA: National Art Education Association, 2007.

Mayer, M. M. "Looking Outside the Frame: Demystifying Museum Education." *Art Education,* 65 no. 4 (2012): 15–18.

McQuade, Christine, and Donald McQuade. *Seeing & Writing*. Boston, MA. Bedford/St. Martin, 2000.

Murphy, Shannon. December 6, 2012. *Tableaux Vivant: History and Practice*. https://artmuseum teaching.com/2012/12/06/tableaux-vivant-history-and-practice/

Obrist, Hans Ulrich. *Do It: The Compendium*. New York: Independent Curators International, 2013.

Padgett, Ron. *The Teachers & Writers Handbook of Poetic Forms*. New York: Teachers & Writers Collaborative, 2000.

Piazza, Carolyn L. *Multiple Forms of Literacy: Teaching Literacy and the Arts*. Upper Saddle River, NJ: Prentice-Hall, 1999.

Project Zero, http://www.pz.harvard.edu/projects/visible-thinking

Rand, Judy. January. "The 227-Mile Museum, or, Why We Need a Visitors' Bill of Rights." *Curator: The Museum Journal,* 44, no. 1 (2001): 7–14.

Ron Ritchhart. "Cultivating a Culture of Thinking in Museums," *Journal of Museum Education* 32, no. 2 (summer 2007): 137–54. http://www.ronritchhart.com/Papers_files/JME07_Ritchhart .pdf

Ritchart, Ron, Mark Church, and Karen Morrison. *Making Thinking Visible: How to Promote Engagement, Understanding, and Independence for All Learners*. San Francisco, CA: Jossey-Bass, 2011.

Samis, Peter, and Mimi Michaelson. *Creating the Visitor Centered Museum*. New York: Routledge, 2017.

Schmidt, Laurel. *Classroom Confidential: The 12 Secrets of Great Teachers*. Portsmouth, NH: Heinemann, 2004.

Shulman Herz, Rebecca. *Looking at Art in the Classroom: Art Investigations from the Guggenheim Museum*. New York: Teachers College Press, 2010.

Simon, Nina. *The Participatory Museum*. Santa Cruz, CA: Museum 2.0, 2010.

Smith, Nancy, and the Drawing Study Group. *Observation Drawing with Children*. New York: Teachers College Press, 1998.

Spolin, Viola. *Improvisation for the Theater, Third Edition*. Evanston, IL: Northwestern University Press, 1999.

Walsh-Piper, Kathleen. *Image to Word: Art and Creative Writing*. Lanham, MD: Scarecrow Press, 2002.

Weisberg, Shelley Kruger. 2006. *Museum Movement Techniques*. Lanham, MD: AltaMira.

Wold, Milo, Gary Martin, James Miller, and Edmund Cykler. *An Introduction to Music and Art in the Western World, Tenth Edition*. Dubuque, IA: Brown and Benchmark, 1996.

Index

as seated, *19*; toolkit of, 74. *See also* drawing
    activities; writing activities
participatory activities, 23–24, *24*
Passage, 116
The Peasant Wedding, 70–71
percussion instruments, 98, *98*
Pereda, Antonio de, 67, 117
Peter Fischli David Weiss: How to Work Better, 68,
    78–79
Pew Research Center, 107
Philadelphia Museum of Art, 71
physical comfort, 20–21
Pica, Amalia, *82*, *81*
Picasso, Pablo, *56*, 56–57, 61, *62*, *63*, 97
Pich, Soheap, 68
Pier 40, 118–20, *119*
Pijbes, Wim, 48
Pissarro, Camille, 30, *30*
place, focus on, 105–6
Place Vintimille, 106
planning, 7–11
playful activities, 25
Pollock, Jackson, 67, 98
popular opposites, 79
postcard reflections activity, 43
postcards home activity, 43
Poughkeepsie, New York, 76–77, 131n7
priming, 19–20
printmaking tools, 68
Prismacolor Art Stix, 48
private space, 22
problematizing, 57, 59
professional development, 7–11, *88*, 135n1
Project Zero, 41–42
props, touch objects and: close observation and,
    66–67; contemporary artists and, 68–69;
    materials and, 68–69; natural forms and, 66–67;
    overview of, 61–72, *62*, *63*, *64*, *65*, *66*, *68*, *69*,
    70, *71*; smell and, *70*, 70–71; tactile museums,
    71, 71–72; tools of artist as, 67–68, *68*
public space, 22

Qiu Zhijie, 57, *58*
questions, 9

Rand, Judy, 17–18
Randi Korn and Associates, 31
Red Poppy, 103
reflection: by educators, 26; group, 135n3; postcard
    activity, 43; on tours, 25, 26, 122, 135n3
Renoir, Pierre-Auguste, 35, *36*, *37*, 63, *64*
reporter, 65, *65*
reproduction/original activity, 103
responses, 9–10, 25
Rijksmuseum, 48, 113

Ring Around the Roses, 85
Rodin Museum, 71
Rome, Italy, 103
Ropeik, Rachel, 25
rounds, 67
Rousseau, Henri, *87*, 98
Russian art, 66

Sacchi/Sacks paintings, 69
Saltz, Jerry, 29
schmootz, 120
Schönberg, Arnold, 93, 95
school, living pictures at, 89
school-based teachers, 4
science, 5–6
scissors, collage without, 73, *74*
Scriabin, Alexander, 95
sculpture, 50, *50*, 89. *See also* collage, sculpture,
    and manipulatives; linear sculpture/abstraction
see-think-wonder activity, 41
Self-Adhesive Laminating Sheets, 73, 128n11
Seow, Ai Wee, 108, 134n8
sequencing, 8–9
Seurat, Georges, 89, 100–101
Several Circles, 75
Shahn, Ben, 115
sharing, 25, 113
Simon, Nina, 3
Singapore, 22
smartphones/audio recording, 112
smartphones/photos, 110–12, *111*
smell, 70, 70–71
Smith, David, 76–77
Smithsonian Institution, 83
snapshot, 38–39
social studies, 5
Socrates, 17
Sollins, Susan, xiv, 83
Solomon R. Guggenheim Museum, xiii–xvi, *xv*, 3,
    4, 39, 101–2; abstraction creation at, 90; audio
    recording and editing at, 113; collaboration of,
    7–11; *Drawing the Guggenheim* of, *53*, 53–54;
    Gutai: Splendid Playground mounted by, 116;
    I Used to Think . . . , Now I Think . . . activity
    used by, 41–42; Ko at, 135n7; Latin America art
    at, 57, 59; Learning Through Art of, 31; Mir at,
    134n1; on Model Magic, 21; multimedia guide
    of, 108; problematizing used by, 57, 59; *Under
    the Same Sun: Art from Latin America Today* on
    view in, 115–16; Smith retrospective, 76–77;
    Teaching Literacy Through Art, 2002-2006 by, 31;
    Teen Night at, 110. *See also* drawing; drawing
    activities; props, touch objects and
Sontag, Susan, 110
Sophocles, 13

Wright, Frank Lloyd, 53–54, 79
writing activities, 118; before and after as, 39;
adults collaborating on, *38*; callouts as, 32–33,
33; character development as, 34–35; cinquains
as, 38–39; collaborative poetry as, 37–38, *38*;
compare and contrast as, 42; concrete poetry
as, 34; considered impressions as, 42–43; daily
schedule as, 35, *36*, *37*; diaries as, 35; first
impressions as, 42–43; five senses exquisite
corpse as, 34; getting inside as, 39; haiku as,
38; I Used to Think . . . , Now I Think . . . as,
41–42; journals as, 35; leading with title as, 39,
40; manifestos as, 42; overview of, 29–44, *30*,
31, *32*, *33*, *36*, *37*, *38*, *40*; postcard reflections as,
43; postcards home as, 43; see-think-wonder
as, 41; thought bubbles as, 32–33, *33*; untitled
no more as, 39; verbal description as, 43–44;
whip-around as, 39, 41; writing dialogue as, 35
writing dialogue, 35

Yardsticks: Children in the Classroom Ages 4–14
(Wood), 22
Yenawine, Philip, 83
Yesterday, 57
Yi, Anicka, 70
youth, with disabilities, 4

About the Author

Figure 14.1 Sharon Vatsky, director of school and family programs, Solomon R. Guggenheim Museum.
PHOTO: KRIS MCKAY

Sharon Vatsky, director of school and family programs at the Solomon. R. Guggenheim Museum, oversees programs for youth, families, and teachers. She brings her experience as a lifelong arts educator, museum educator, and artist to considering the role of multimodal explorations in responding to works of art.

She has conducted workshops for teachers and museum educators at universities and art museums in the United States and internationally, and has taught graduate level courses in museum education at the City University of New York and Teachers College, Columbia University, as well as undergraduate courses in drawing, painting, design, art history, and arts education.

Prior to joining the Guggenheim in 2000, she was curator of education at the Queens Museum in New York for more than a decade.